Strategy and the **Fat Smoker**

"David has a knack of explaining what is really going on around us in our business life in a way which brings clarity and insight to the issues. His long experience in the professional services sector shines through. David doesn't let anyone off the hook in his evaluation of where professional service firms often go wrong. He forces us to confront the real issues of lack of resolve, leadership, values and trust which so often hold firms back. This is a book which all those with an interest in how professional service firms should be managed and led should read."

—DAVID MORLEY, MANAGING PARTNER, ALLEN & OVERY

"David Maister is both smart and wise in this book. He employs common-sense but rarely-encountered lessons from the personal lives of humans to inform the strategy and management of professional services firms."

—TOM DAVENPORT, PROFESSOR AND DIRECTOR OF RESEARCH, BABSON EXECUTIVE EDUCATION, BABSON COLLEGE, AUTHOR OF *THINKING FOR A LIVING*

"With liberal doses of insight and humor, Maister demonstrates that strategy cannot and should not be reduced to a formula. This book shows us that what are critical are the human elements of leadership, motivation and personal fulfillment."

—JEFF SWYSTUN, DIRECTOR OF GLOBAL COMMUNICATIONS, DDB WORLDWIDE

"This is an inspirational collection of articles, full of insights and ideas you want to use at the first opportunity or send to your colleagues. A thoroughly rewarding read and certainly good for you."

—MARK READ, DIRECTOR OF STRATEGY, WPP

STRATEGY

AND THE

FAT SMOKER

DOING WHAT'S OBVIOUS BUT NOT EASY

DAVID MAISTER

The Spangle Press ·❖ *Boston, Massachusetts*

Published by The Spangle Press
90 Commonwealth Avenue
Boston, MA 02116, USA
1-617-933-9812 or toll free: 1-866-530-6852

Printed in the United States of America.

Design: stresslimitdesign

10 9 8 7 6 5 4 3 2 1

Library of Congress Control Number: 2007936862

ISBN: 978-09798457-1-0

This book is also available as an e-book at online bookstores.

Bulk discounts may be available for quantity purchases used for
sales promotions, employee premiums, or educational purposes.
Please email our special sales department at *orders@spanglepress.com.*

TO KATHY

CONTENTS

Introduction

As I explain in the title chapter of this book, we often (or even usually) know what we *should be* doing in both personal and professional life. We also know *why* we should be doing it and (often) *how* to do it. Figuring all that out is not too difficult.

What is very hard is actually doing what you know to be good for you in the long-run, in spite of short-run temptations.

The same is true for organizations. In 2000, Pfeffer and Sutton explored the gap between knowing what to do and actually doing it in a terrific book called ***The Knowing-Doing Gap***. I explore the same phenomenon, but from different perspectives.

In the past two-and-a-half decades, I have been trusted to see a large number of strategic plans from a wide variety of professional firms around the world, including direct competitors. What is immediately noteworthy is how similar (if not identical) they all are.

This is not because anyone is being stupid, but because everyone is smart. Every competitor is smart enough to analyze the market and spot which sectors are growing and which are in decline. Few competitors get it wrong. Everyone—absolutely everyone—can see which services and products are "hot" and which are becoming commodities.

What is more, everyone understands the basics of business success: provide outstanding client service, act like team players, provide a good place to work, invest in your future. No sensible firm (or person) would enunciate a strategy that advocated anything else.

The words and slogans may change over the years (from "Outstanding Client Care," to "Trusted Advisor," to "Loyalty" or "Client-Centricity," for example), but the underlying ideas remain the same around the world, over time, and from competitor to competitor.

However, just because something is *obvious* doesn't make it *easy*. Real strategy lies not in figuring out what to do, but in devising ways to ensure that, compared to others, we actually do more of what everybody knows they should do.

This simple insight, if accepted, has profound implications for:

1. how organizations should think about **strategy**

2. how they should think about **clients**, marketing, and selling

3. how they should think about **management**

As a general outline, that's how this book is organized.

Chapters 1 through 5 are explicitly about strategy: what strategy is and how individuals and organizations should go about developing their strategies.

> **Real strategy lies not in figuring out ... but in ...nsure ...red to ...tually ...what ...they ...d do.**

Chapters 6 through 8 dig more deeply into an aspect of strategy frequently advocated but seldom achieved: excellence in client relationships.

Chapters 9 through 14 are about management: how organizations can run themselves to overcome the barriers and temptations of the Fat Smoker syndrome.

In the final section "Putting it Together,"—chapters 15 through 19—I examine some of the barriers to organizational cohesion, the policies of some widely admired firms and, finally, offer some summary thoughts about what it takes to stay true to your strategic goals and ambitions.

The chapters in this book were written (and made available on my website) between 2005 and 2007. However, with one or two exceptions, this book represents their first appearance in print. While originally written as separate articles, I have tried here to integrate my arguments into a coherent flow. Nevertheless, it does not have to be read at one sitting from beginning to end. Feel free to "dip into" the book at any point, according to the sections and chapters that seem of greatest interest to you.

Part One: **Strategy**

CHAPTER 1

Strategy and the **Fat Smoker**

This title chapter for the book establishes the themes that I will explore throughout the book. The key lesson is that, individually and collectively, knowing that something is good for us is not necessarily a predictor that we are going to do it. This has many implications for careers and company strategy; in particular, the conclusion that the necessary outcome of strategic planning processes is not analytical insight, but greater resolve.

Much of what individuals and firms do in the name of strategic planning is a complete waste of time and about as effective as making New Year's resolutions. The reasons are the same in both situations. Personally and professionally, we already know that we should do: lose weight, give up smoking, and exercise more. In business, strategic plans are also stuffed with familiar goals: build client relationships, act like team players, and provide fulfilling, motivating careers.

We want the benefits of these things. We know *what* to do, we know *why* we should do it, and we know *how* to do it. Yet most businesses and individuals don't do what's good for them.

The problem is that many change efforts are based on the

> **We know what to do, we know why we should do it, and we know how to do it. Yet most businesses and individuals don't do what's good for them.**

assumption that all you have to do is explain to people that their lives could be better, convince them that the goals are worth going for, and show them how to do it.

But this assumption is patently false. If it were true, there would be no drug addicts, no alcoholics, or bad marriages in the world. "Oh, I see, this behavior's not good for me? Ah well then, I'll stop, of course!" What nonsense!

And yet strategic plans and annual speeches by CEOs, managing partners, management consultants, and others continue to adopt this same useless structure: "Look at how fabulous it would be if you were a fit, nonsmoking exerciser, David!" My usual response? "True, but please shut up and go away."

And that's the response of most audiences to the manager's or consultant's latest vision or strategy: "We knew all this a long time ago. Why don't you ask us why we don't do it?"

Now *there's* an interesting question!

WHY WE **DON'T DO IT**

The primary reason we do not work at behaviors which we know we need to improve is that the rewards (and pleasure) are in the future; the disruption, discomfort and discipline needed to get there are immediate.

To reach our goals, we must first change our lifestyle and our daily habits *now*. Then we must summon the courage to *keep up* the new habits and not yield to all the old familiar temptations. Then, and only then, we get the benefits *later*.

As human beings, we are not good at delayed gratification. We start self-improvement programs with good intentions, but if they don't pay off immediately, or if a temptation to depart from the program arises, we abandon our efforts completely—until the next time we *pretend* to be on the program.

> The rewards (and pleasure) are in the future; the disruption, discomfort and discipline needed to get there are immediate.

That's our pattern. Try a little, succumb to temptation, and give up. Repeat until totally frustrated. Unfortunately, there is rarely, if ever, a benefit from dabbling or trying only a little.

You can't get half the benefits of a better marriage by cutting out half your affairs, cure half the problems of alcoholism by cutting out half the drinks or reduce the risks of lung cancer by cutting out half the cigarettes.

So it is with business strategy: You can't achieve a competitive differentiation through things you do "reasonably well, most of the time." You not only cannot dabble, but you also cannot have short-term strategies (an oxymoron, if ever there was one). The pursuit of short-term goals is inherently anti-strategic and self-defeating.

As Jean Nidech (the founder of Weight Watchers) believed, the pursuit of quick weight loss is always self-defeating and ill-advised. If you don't understand from the beginning that you have to change your lifestyle, now and forever, then you are wasting your time. Any initial weight you lose will be put right back on.

What's more, repeated short-lived efforts at weight loss are actually detrimental to long-term success since, among other reasons, they breed cynicism and the attitude of "I can't do this. I've tried and failed before."

Millions of people and countless businesses have proved her insight exactly correct. You are either seriously on the program, really living what you have chosen, or you are wasting your time.

STRATEGY IS THE DIET,
NOT THE GOAL

Debating whether it is more beneficial to lose weight, give up smoking, stop drinking, or start exercising is a fruitless process if you

> You can't achieve a competitive differentiation through things you do "reasonably well, most of the time."

lack the discipline to do what each specific goal requires. The only meaningful debate is which diet you are really ready to get on.

Giving up smoking may be better for you (or a better competitive strategy), but if you're not willing to make the changes that that specific goal requires, its relative importance is irrelevant.

The same is true in business. Discussing "strengths, weaknesses, opportunities and threats" (to take only the oldest and most familiar of the strategic planning exercises) is fun, but gets nowhere near the real questions.

Improving the quality of the analysis is not where the problem lies. The necessary outcome of strategic planning is not *analytical insight* but *resolve*.

The essential questions of strategy are these: "Which of our habits are we *really* prepared to change, permanently and forever? Which lifestyle changes are we *really* prepared to make? What issues are we *really* ready to tackle?"

Now *that's* a different tone of conversation and discussion (and the reason the real debate is so often avoided). Discussing goals is stimulating, inspiring, and energizing. But it feels tough, awkward, annoying, frightening, and completely unpleasant to discuss the discipline needed to reach those goals.

AN **ILLUSTRATION**

As an example, consider the familiar strategic topic of aiming for competitive differentiation through excellence in client service. Here are three (real-world) examples of programs to achieve this goal:

1) Once a quarter, the chief executive of the firm sends an email to *all* active clients (without consulting the lead people serving those clients), asking them to click on one of three buttons in the email: *green* if

The necessary outcome of strategic planning is not analytical insight but resolve.

they are satisfied with the way their work is being handled, *amber* if they have some concerns and *red* if they are unhappy.

The chief executive personally reviews all the email replies every day, following up on every single one that is not a green. Every quarter, the group averages on this score are published for each operating unit within the firm (every office, every discipline area) and distributed to everyone in the organization. So, each quarter, even the mailroom clerks can see how well each of the company's groups is doing on client satisfaction.

2) At compensation-setting time, the relevant senior management group conducts a phone or face-to-face interview with every client served by each partner in the last year (or a scientifically chosen random sample if the number of clients is too high to be practical).

These client assessments carry a significant (40 to 60 percent) weighting in pay. You can't get paid for selling or increasing volume unless it is more volume of highly satisfied clients. There is no reward for more volume of only moderately satisfied clients.

3) The organization adopts and publicizes an unconditional satisfaction guarantee, allowing disappointed clients to pay only what they thought the work was worth.

These are just three examples of how to enforce the same strategic idea. Other ideas may be superior. Like any diet, substitutes are allowed. No one diet idea is free of flaws or drawbacks. The best diet for you is the one you will stick to.

> **No one diet idea is free of flaws or drawbacks. The best diet for you is the one you will stick to.**

Your firm needs to debate the following questions if you *really* want to pursue this or any other strategic goal:

- Which "diet," if integrated into the normal running of the firm, would actually get us to perform at the level required to achieve the benefits we seek?

- Which would we be prepared to adopt as a central part of our regular lifestyle?

- If we don't like any of these diets, can we think of another that will have as much force as these, but that we could live with more easily?

If there is no specific diet that all your people can agree to follow, then you must conclude that you are not really willing or able to pursue that strategic goal.

There is no shame in aiming for competence if you are unwilling to pay the price for excellence. But don't try to mislead clients, staff, colleagues or yourself with time-wasting, demoralizing attempts to convince them that you are actually committed to pursuing the goal.

WHAT GETS PEOPLE **ON THE DIET?**

If all business improvement is like curing a fat smoker or helping an alcoholic recover, then what actually motivates people and organizations to change?

> There is no shame in aiming for competence if you are unwilling to pay the price for excellence. But don't try to mislead clients, staff, colleagues or yourself.

We all know the main thing that works: a major crisis! If revenues drop off sharply, it's amazing how quickly businesses can act to deal with known inefficiencies and bad habits they could have tackled years ago.

And when the first heart attack comes, it's amazing how many people suddenly find the self-discipline to start living right.

That's close to what happened to me. Until March 2005, I was a fat smoker. I had been overweight for most of my life and smoked a pack a day for thirty-seven years. I don't say that as a confession. I never pretended that getting fit was my strategy.

Then, a variety of medical conditions landed me in the hospital with a kidney malfunction. In the five months that followed, I stopped smoking, started exercising and lost thirty pounds.

This was all wonderful news for me and an amazing and welcome surprise to my family and friends, but a depressing conclusion for any theory of change.

Do people and institutions really have to wait until something very serious happens before they will fix things they have known about for years? Isn't there any hope of a better way?

Here are some of the few things we know about persuading people to change before the heart attack comes:

1. It's about a Permanent Change in Lifestyle

A major source of failure in implementing sensible business strategies is that we underestimate how much effort is truly required to bring about significant improvement.

Individuals and organizations frequently fail to incorporate the new activities into their daily lives. Strategic actions are viewed as special, separate events rather than regular business activities. In other words, there's real life, and then there's the diet.

Viewed that way, all improvement programs are doomed to failure. As my trainer has pointed out, you don't really get the sustained benefits of exercise until it has become as routine and is as natural as brushing your teeth and taking a shower each day.

Do people and institutions really have to wait until something very serious happens before they will fix things they have known about for years?

Anything less than that will jeopardize any short-term gains you may obtain with bursts of activity. It's about routines, not special events.

2. You Must Change the Scorecards

If strategy is to be lived and achieved, is must be publicly tracked, measured and monitored. If you are trying to lose weight, you must get on the scales regularly. Otherwise, you may fool yourself into thinking you are progressing. Even if you weigh yourself regularly but keep the results private, you still escape accountability. How much more forceful it would be if you let your spouse see, each time, what you weigh! Or better yet, what about letting your children monitor your progress?

We all forgive ourselves too easily. We all find it quite easy to live with guilt. Even a high level of guilt doesn't always change people. However, embarrassment, even in small doses, can be far more effective.

So it is in professional life. When I was a teacher at the Harvard Business School (HBS), students evaluated every course at the end of every semester, and the results were published to everyone on campus. There was no doubt at *that* institution as to what the strategy was!

3. Leadership: Get Serious, or Get Out of the Way

Organizations often rush to figure out how the troops need to change in order to live the new standards. However, this is not the first task. Perhaps the single biggest difficulty in getting an organization's members to stick to the diet is convincing them that top management really wants them to.

> **Even a high level of guilt doesn't always change people. However, embarrassment, even in small doses, can be far more effective.**

For example, if a group within the firm faces a choice between a lesser volume of high-quality work and a greater volume of "acceptable-quality" work, it is critical that they understand without ambiguity what choice firm leaders wish them to make. If they believe that management, when push comes to shove, wants the second alternative, they will never stretch to engage in strategic behaviors themselves.

If an organization's leaders want their people to believe that a new strategy is being followed, they must establish credibility by proving that they are prepared to change themselves: how they act, measure, and reward.

I can share countless examples of failure to do this. I was asked by one firm to run a program for its middle managers on how to be more effective as managers, but my instructions included this statement: "Please don't raise the topic of how well we ourselves manage these middle managers. We're not ready to discuss the terrible job we do at that. Keep their attention on what *they* could do better. We want them to change first."

Can you imagine a process less likely to get the people in the organization to actually aspire to higher standards? (I am somewhat ashamed to report that I did continue with that assignment, and it proved to be as ineffective as I feared. Nowadays, I try very hard to avoid such work. See chapter 10 on "Why (Most) Training is Useless.")

A similar event happened when I was asked to moderate a discussion in a firm that wanted the people in its different regions to work for the good of the institution, not just their own region. Unfortunately, as I led this discussion, the CEO at the back of the room became more and more agitated.

I later found out that he had turned to his second in command and said, "This guy keeps talking about what we in management need to change to become a one-firm firm. We wanted him to talk about what the people out in the

> **Leaders must establish credibility by proving that they are prepared to change themselves: how they act, measure, and reward.**

field need to do." Not surprisingly, the group never achieved collaboration, and I was never invited back to that firm!

This story illustrates, by the way, the fatal flaw in relying too heavily on using outside speakers and consultants. Whether or not they are convincing, educational or inspirational, the question on the audience's mind is "Do our leaders believe this and are they actually going to run the firm that way?"

All too often, the audience is given no evidence of the firm's leadership's commitment to the ideas, and the whole exercise becomes a waste of money and time. I have been told often that people's response to my presentations is, "This all makes terrific sense, but there's no way we'll ever do these things around here."

If people are to make the right strategic decision in every location of the firm, in every operating group, and at every level, then they must absolutely *trust* that management will back them up and reward them (or at least not punish them) for acting in accordance with the declared strategy. A large part of *really* bringing about strategic change is designing some action or new system that visibly, inescapably, and irreversibly commits top management to the strategy.

I have sometimes asked firm leaders whether they are willing to announce to their people, right up front, that they will resign their roles if measurable progress is not made on the strategic plans they advocate. Such a commitment has had a dramatic impact where it has been made.

> **A large part of really bringing about strategic change is designing some action or new system that visibly, inescapably, and irreversibly commits top management to the strategy.**

4. Principles Are More Effective Than Tactics

Since successful implementation of a strategy requires both sustained commitment over time and broad participation across the whole organization, strategies in business, like diets and alcohol recovery, are implemented much more effectively when the ideas are presented as matters of principle, not just as matters of expediency.

If strategic rules are justified only in terms of outcomes ("Treating employees well gets us more money"), the diet will always be seen as a punishment on the way to an uncertain and possibly unattainable reward. Accordingly, it will always be resented.

If, however, the diet achieves the force of moral principle ("Treating clients and employees with respect is the right thing to do"), the odds are significantly higher that successful implementation will be achieved. Managers who get things done are people who are viewed as having an ideology. Their people believe that they believe in something.

This is because buy-in and excellent implementation result from a sense of not wanting to let people down. My trainer reports that some of his clients tell him that they keep up their exercise programs between meetings because they "don't want to disappoint him."

5. People Must Volunteer

Even though it is the leader's job to offer an ideology around which people can rally, it is by itself only a first step. A self-improvement program is successful and sustainable only when the individual chooses to do it for himself, not for a spouse, children, or others.

The motivation must be intrinsic, because the essence of successful strategic change is not technique, but *will*. If you prefer, you can call it determination, commitment, or resolve.

To achieve any goal, you must really *want* the goal. Common questions arise in discussions about strategies and strategic change: "Do we have to do this?" "Why, when

> **Strategies in business, are implemented much more effectively when the ideas are presented as matters of principle, not just expediency.**

things are going so well, do we need to invite more discipline into our lives?"

The answer, of course, is that you don't *have* to do anything you don't want to do. Strategy in a professional business is a choice that each individual has to make about whether he or she wants to put more effort into her life and career in order to get somewhere new. (See chapter 3.)

In professional firms, it is dangerous to assume that every person shares this choice. That's why most firms (and most individuals) don't achieve their strategies: not everyone in the firm actually wants to try that hard. They will *say* they want to be the clear market leader in their field; they are just not willing to do what that takes.

As I mentioned earlier, it's a valid choice. After all, I was a fat smoker for thirty-seven years and felt I had the right to remain so. For me and for others, the single biggest barrier to making change is the feeling that "it's OK so far." People don't disagree that the future state of being a nonsmoker would be beneficial, but they resist when they are told that they *have* to do it.

One of a leader's roles is to act as a coach, drawing people's attention to imperfections in the status quo (i.e., creating dissatisfaction), asking whether things could actually be better, and questioning whether the desired change is both achievable and desirable. But it's subtle stuff—the leader must be skilled in not only knowing the answers to these questions, but also in helping others think them through to a personal conclusion. (See chapter 11, "A Great Coach in Action.")

6. People Must Get On or Off the Bus

> **The single biggest barrier to making change is the feeling that "it's OK so far."**

Every individual can, and must, make a personal choice. But then the organization must decide how to respond to those individual choices. For an organization, strategy cannot be what "most of us, most of the time" do. You'll never be good enough as a firm if participation in your firm's definition of excellence is optional.

If a number of top people have plainly not signed up for the journey or are clearly not true believers, no number of systems or amount of inspired speechmaking will transport the organization there. In professional firms, new strategies may result in senior people leaving, as well as new people coming in. Jim Collins, in **Good to Great**, calls this "getting the right people on and off the bus," and identifies it as the first step in all programs for strategic greatness.

Everyone in the organization has to decide if they want to try hard enough to sacrifice some of the present to achieve a better tomorrow. They may do so if they believe that the effort is serious. They definitely will not if they think those at the top are undecided or divided.

Professional firms are afraid of this conclusion. They try to work around the skeptics, the nonbelievers, and the nonparticipants in their senior ranks, preferring to hold on to revenue volume rather than put together a senior team whose members are equally committed to reaching. That's fine, but you can't call it strategy.

As all married people who diet know, it's hard enough to stay the course and resist temptation when you are both attempting to do the right thing. It's well nigh impossible if those around you continue to indulge and tempt you with food, alcohol, etc.

Similarly, organizations must jointly endeavor to resist temptations that could deter them from their course. Again, we cannot force others to do what we want. We can, however, protect those who have chosen to participate; doing so may require ridding the firm of those who refuse to come on board.

Strategy cannot be what "most of us, most of the time" do.

People have a desperate need for the mutual support (and social structure) that comes from joining in a common cause. They need to help each other through the tough times ("Come on, let's do it one more time!") instead of being part of a forgiving culture that keeps discouraging extra effort ("Oh, that's OK, you can skip exercise today. You deserve a break.").

That's why other researchers and I continually rediscover that the most successful organizations have an ideology. There *is* a McKinsey way, a Goldman Sachs approach, and a Bain philosophy, to cite only three examples of firms with strong ideologies, clear strategies, and the financial success to match.

At these firms, if you don't subscribe to the ideology, you don't stay and argue or act as a silent dissenter. You walk. Or, eventually, you'll be asked to walk.

MANAGING THE **PROCESS OF CHANGE**

None of this is meant to imply that firms must change overnight. Like alcoholic recovery, it is a process that requires you to first make a lifetime commitment, and then take it one day at time.

Once we know what the agreed-upon diet is, there is a need for skilled coaching in leading individuals and teams through the struggle to attain the goals they have committed to.

The key is to manage with a philosophy of "It's OK to stumble; it's only a sin if you don't get back on the program." The primary goal of the beginning stage of a change program is to get people to believe that it *is* doable and that all we are asking is that they try. This means early successes.

> People have a desperate need for the mutual support (and social structure) that comes from joining in a common cause.

All that wise leaders (and good trainers) talk about is the next small step. And they enthusiastically celebrate each small accomplishment. They focus on requiring improvement, not on requiring excellence. "As long as you are improving, you're with the program and one of us!"

Managing a weight-loss program means you *stop* talking about the ultimate goal. If you keep reminding me that I need to lose fifty pounds, it is as likely to backfire and make me give up as it is to energize me.

But what if someone says to me: "Let's just focus on losing one pound in a week, David. Do you think you can do that? *That* doesn't sound impossible, does it?" My reaction to that will be a lot different. Of course, one pound a week *is* fifty pounds in a year. An alcoholic is daunted by a lifetime of abstinence, but he or she can manage, just for today, not to drink just for one day.

First you establish what is important; then you get people to do a little of it, then a little more. It is commitment to a process of *continually improving things that matter.* I describe this as a managerial style of insistent patience: "Rome wasn't built in a day, but we *are* building Rome."

Encouragement is an essential ingredient in the recipe. When I began exercising, it was sobering to realize how much I needed my trainer's words ("Good, good, David") when I had just been able to complete an exercise for the first time. At one level, I knew I was pathetically bad, but it really did help to hear his constant encouragement: "You're doing much better, David. You may not be able to feel it, but as a trainer I can see it."

I don't know how much of his encouragement was false optimism or a well-practiced mind game. But, as every good trainer knows, that's the point. We *all* need to play mind games with ourselves when we struggle to build new

Managing a weight-loss program means you stop talking about the ultimate goal. If you keep reminding me that I need to lose fifty pounds, it is as likely to backfire and make me give up as it is to energize me.

achievements and habits into our lives. ("If I can just finish this first one, I'll reward myself with a break.")

It also means making a game of strategic programs. Educated professionals may scoff, but it's profoundly rooted in the human psyche that making a game of something helps to sustain strenuous effort.

The importance of games explains all the hoopla of various strategic initiatives such as "Six Sigma," "quality is free," and similar fads, business jargon, prizes, rewards, and "black belt" recognition programs. They work, even among cynical people, because they make a "mind game" of the whole thing, creating a framework on which to hang the mind-distracting habits. ("If I can just do this one thing, I can make it. If I change the way I do that, I will be better able to stick with the rest of it.")

Good trainers know that life-changing improvement can and does fail by rushing to either of the two extremes. The first extreme establishes overly ambitious or time-consuming improvement goals, leading to frustration and abandonment of the program. The other extreme fails to establish any pressure to improve, allowing people to pretend that they plan to get on the program, but just not today.

The good news in all of this is that, in the world at large, there is experience in helping people make significant improvement in their lives. There *are* well-documented methodologies; they are just not the ones we usually associate with the business world.

If we are prepared to rethink how we view strategy and business life, then people can achieve things they never thought possible. If I can become a fitter, nonsmoking exerciser, there's truly no limit!

CHAPTER TWO

Strategy Means **Saying "No"**

In the previous chapter, I argued that what's hard about a diet and exercise program is having the courage and self-discipline to stick to what you have chosen. This chapter explores that insight more deeply, offering the view that, as hard as it is to do, strategy is deciding whose business you are going to turn away.

I was helping a prominent global company explore the strategy of achieving high levels of client service. We were discussing ways of investing resources and redesigning processes to accomplish this goal. The longer the discussion continued, the more uncomfortable some members of the organization became.

"But what about the clients and customers who don't want all this high-touch contact?" they asked me. "What are we supposed to do with them? Won't we scare away a significant portion of our current customer base by doing things they don't want?"

"Yes, you will," I replied. "A strategy is not just choosing a target market, but actually designing

> A strategy is not just choosing a target market, but actually designing an operation that will consistently deliver the superior client benefits you claim to provide.

an operation that will consistently deliver the superior client benefits you claim to provide.

"However, each decision you make to be more effective at delivering the preferences of those you target will (inevitably, inescapably, unavoidably) make you less attractive to clients or market segments that look for different benefits.

"But consider the alternative," I continued. "You could design your operations to meet a wide variety of preferences and needs, serving each client or customer group differently, according to its individual wishes.

"Your market appeal will then come down to 'tell us what you want us to do for you and we'll do that. We'll do something different for other people tomorrow!'

"You may get by with this approach, but you will be unlikely to achieve a competitive differentiation or reputation, except as people who, as long as they are getting paid, will do anything for anyone. Which is not an image I think you want to have."

Finally, someone said out loud what was on everybody's mind: "But do we have the courage to turn away business? Do we really have the confidence to tell paying customers that we are not right for them?"

My answer? "Not only should you do that, but the *only* way you *can* achieve any strategic distinction is to do that. Strategy is deciding whose business you are going to turn away."

THE FOCUSED FACTORY

One of the first lessons I was taught at Harvard Business School in the 1970s was Wickham Skinner's principle of the "focused factory." No operation, Professor Skinner pointed out, can be

ing simultaneously.

deciding
s you are
irn away.

An operation designed to provide the highest quality is unlikely to be the one that achieves the lowest cost, and one that can respond to a wide variety of customized requests is be unlikely to provide fast response and turnaround. Any business that tries to deliver all four virtues of quality, cost, variety, and speed is doomed to failure.

This is not just an operational point, but a marketing one. To be differentiated in the eyes of the marketplace, you have to be known for something in particular. It's not enough just to be known. (That's name awareness, which is not the same thing as being seen as differentiated). And you can't have a reputation for being something specific if you only do it occasionally.

The very essence of having a strategy is being *selective* about choosing the criteria on which a firm wishes to compete, and then being creative and disciplined in designing an operation that is finely tuned to deliver those *particular virtues*.

Consider McDonalds. For any customer who truly places a premium on low cost and speed, McDonalds is hard to beat because it has been optimized around a clear market positioning.

However, if someone were to walk into a McDonald's and say, "I feel like having a pizza today," the service provider would not reply "Sure. That will increase our revenues. Let me shut down the grill and make you one."

Instead, the reply would be, "I'm sorry, but we are not designed to meet every possible need. Perhaps I can help you find somewhere nearby that can give you what you want."

As companies keep discovering to their detriment, it is certain business decay if you try to please all possible market segments. The broader the group of clients to which you try to appeal, or the wider the range of services you try to provide, the less customized your operation can be to each segment within that group.

If you never say "no," you will just be one more undifferentiated firm, trying to do a little bit of

> **As companies keep discovering to their detriment, it is certain business decay if you try to please all possible market segments.**

everything and, as Skinner pointed out, will almost certainly be superb at none of them.

WHY IT'S HARD

As obvious as this all may seem, translating it into reality can be very difficult. The practical reality of most businesses is that they find it very difficult to say "no" to a revenue-generating opportunity.

As Dick Tyler, managing partner of UK law firm CMS Cameron McKenna, says, "The hardest thing in the world for most professionals to do is to turn work away. It offends our desperate desire to be liked by everyone, and plays to insecurity that afflicts even the best of us. The moment we aren't worked off our feet, we think we'll never work again."

The situation has been made worse by many firms' explicit (if misguided) efforts to transform themselves into "one-stop shopping" operations with extensive efforts at cross-selling additional services to clients and customers.

Too many firms have made growth and size, rather than differentiation, their strategic priority. Instead of identifying and executing a clear market positioning, many companies and firms have consciously pursued a policy of "If you need it, we can do it!"

Many have learned the costs of doing this—a lack of focus and reputation that, while it helps you get *more* business, may actively work to prevent you getting a reputation for being the place to come for the best business—the most attractive work for the most attractive clients.

> **Too many firms have made growth and size, rather than differentiation, their strategic priority.**

Another concept they taught me at business school was "the wheel of retailing." Apparently, it is a common syndrome among new retail stores to begin by establishing a unique positioning in the marketplace, and then succumb to selling an ever-widening range of things to a continually broadening audience.

Eventually, the store ends up looking like every other general store, and is outperformed by new upstarts who go back to the core and establish focused shops with clear, differentiated appeal (and start the cycle all over again).

As this example illustrates, staying focused and true to a strategy has been, and always will be, hard to do.

The hunger for volume (and the use of managerial scorecards that emphasize it) has meant that many individuals and firms are uncomfortable with (or even shocked by) the notion that, to achieve a distinctive strategy, they will need to turn away work that a major competitor may reasonably want to serve.

"Oh, we don't want to take it that far!" they say. "Our strategy is to emphasize certain things, not to exclude others. If a client opportunity comes along outside the strategic areas we have chosen, we'll serve that client. We're under too much fiscal pressure to turn away cash opportunities. Can't we just develop a clear and crisp value proposition and then let the clients decide if they want to pay for it?"

My answer is that you can't get the benefits of a strategy that you don't implement, and half measures are unlikely to work. Strategy is not about understanding something—or planning to get around to it. It's about having the courage to make it happen. You can't let other people, even clients, determine the pace at which you create your distinctiveness.

A PERSONAL **EXPERIENCE**

When I first left my academic post at Harvard Business School and launched my consulting business, I was terrified. For the first time in my life, I had signed an office lease, and hired my first employee.

> You can't get the benefits of a strategy that you don't implement, and half measures are unlikely to work.

I had a dream (more a hope at that stage) that I could distinguish myself from the general mainstream of management consultants by focusing on a particular sector—professional service firms.

However, one of the first phone calls I received was from a car manufacturer who was familiar with some of the work I had done while still a teacher in the more general area of customer service. How would I like, he asked, to provide training in retail customer service to his dealers?

You can see the problem. Did I want the cash? You bet! I was just starting out. But if I spent my time doing generic customer service training for car dealers, I wasn't going to make myself distinctive as a consultant. I would be one more competent guy doing what any number of other people could do.

I had to make a choice. Did I believe in my own strategy and have the courage to spend my time making it a reality, or was I sufficiently insecure to be lured away from my chosen strategy by the promise of cash?

I'm not saying the choice was easy, and I'm not saying that I was or am a better (or nobler) person than anyone because I turned the opportunity down and chose to pursue my differentiation strategy. I *am* saying that facing such decisions is the very essence of what having a strategy is all about. If you don't have the courage, you will never achieve a differentiated strategy.

And, of course, courage is one of the scarcest commodities there is. That's why it's a significant source of competitive advantage!

EXCUSES, EXCUSES

Courage is one of the scarcest commodities there is. That's why it's a significant source of competitive advantage!

Even when people acknowledge this truth, they still come up with many reasons why they think it is unwise (or even forbidden) to say "no."

Many people worry that it would be perceived as being unresponsive, tantamount to being a bad service provider if they were to decline to serve an existing client's new need. They fear criticism if they say, "We don't want to serve you in that additional area."

This fear, however, misses the point. What you say to the client is not "We don't want your additional work" but "We are not your best choice for that new need. We can do it if you insist, but you may be better served to go to a specialist who can focus on providing the particular client benefit you seek."

Worded that way, your statement will likely cement your relationship with that client, not hurt it, because it demonstrates your trustworthiness and your willingness to place the clients' interests ahead of your own short-term gain. If you really believe in the power of relationships, having a select group of key clients who trust you is of vastly greater economic value than having a larger group of clients who are always suspicious of your motives.

Thomas Davenport, author of *Thinking for a Living*, notes, "I've seen a number of cases where turning down business actually helped the firm immediately. For example, when some top consulting firms turn down work because they do not think it can be done effectively without the involvement of the prospective clients' senior management, the client's middle managers will often redesign the assignment and take it upstream to their top managers. So by sticking to its guns, the providing firm gets more business of the kind that it prefers, and impresses the client with its strategic integrity."

Still, many people are unconvinced. "Yes," they observe, "It may be more noble and a good way to earn trust, but doesn't it just allow

Having a select group of key clients who trust you is of vastly greater economic value than having a larger group of clients who are always suspicious of your motives.

a competitor to get his nose under the tent? Once you let a competitor start serving your client, don't you run the risk of that competitor stealing your relationship? Shouldn't you work to keep your competitors out of dealing with your clients?"

The first answer to this is that, even if you tried to pull it off, it would be completely impossible to keep your client away from all other providers. The typical corporation already uses multiple law firms, many consulting firms, many IT providers and numerous marketing communications agencies. The hope, in these and other professions, that you can keep everyone else away is delusional.

Secondly, the truth is that you retain clients' loyalty by serving them superbly, earning their trust and making them want to have a relationship with you above all others. Firms threatened by their clients' potential relationships with other providers appear insecure and unimpressive. Strong, self-confident professional businesses with healthy identities do not try to do everything for their clients. Ask the world's most elite (and profitable) law firms to do a broad range of your legal work, and they will patiently explain that they should only be hired when you truly require the world's experts in their chosen field(s).

The same is true of top consulting firms like McKinsey and Bain. Even if they were to discover the need for training or focus groups in the course of their strategy work, they would likely not offer these services merely to deflect other management consulting firms.

You retain clients' loyalty by serving them superbly, earning their trust and making them want to have a relationship with you above all others.

"Ah, yes," people say, "It's all very well to cite examples like that. But these are established, successful firms. They can afford to say 'no.' We can't."

There's a chicken and an egg problem here. If you can't afford to say 'no' until you are successful and distinguished, then , never be successful and distinguished.

Everyone has an excuse for why he or she cannot make the hard choices, and why he or she needs a special exemption. Small firms claim they should be excused because they are not yet established. Large firms, on the other hand, bemoan the fact that they have a big "factory" of people on the payroll that they have to keep busy.

Young people claim they cannot afford to take risks and be selective because they have student loans and are too junior to decline opportunities. Senior people point to their mortgage obligations, the need to pay their kids' college fees and so on.

Everyone has reasons why it's especially hard for them to be strategic and say no. Most of these "reasons" are really excuses. They reflect risk aversion and a lack of courage.

David C. Baker, who specializes in advising marketing communications firms, puts it this way: "If you are any good at all, eventually you'll have more opportunities than you can handle. Not choosing carefully between those opportunities is far more likely to harm you than the occasional opportunity that slips by because you say 'no.'

"You need to say 'no' to save your energy for the opportunities that are worth pursuing. Entrepreneurs, especially, have a hard time not pursuing any opportunity for learning and stimulation, but the successful ones are really choosy. Don't let panic tempt you."

WHAT DOES MANAGEMENT **REALLY WANT?**

Perhaps the single biggest problem in achieving the implementation of a strategy is the difficulty of ensuring that everyone in the organization understands what the

If you can't afford to say 'no' until you are successful and distinguished, then you'll never be successful and distinguished.

strategy is, and that top management really wants everyone else to follow it.

In the global meeting that I described at the beginning of this article, someone eventually asked, "How can the management of this firm ask me to achieve a distinctive market positioning while simultaneously pressuring me to meet budget numbers? Given a choice, and there is one, what do they really want me to do?"

If the strategy is to become real, then the answer from management must be, "We want both current cash and the benefits of sticking to a strategy. But if it ever becomes a choice, we want you to place execution of our strategy ahead of meeting the budget. Following this rule, and pulling off our strategy, we'll make more money, not less."

The CEO's message needs to be as unambiguous as Warren Buffet's description (to a U.S. Senate subcommittee) of his managerial philosophy: "Make an honest mistake and I will be understanding, but lose the reputation of the enterprise and I will be ruthless."

Even the most senior vice-presidents and partners indicate that they do not think the new strategies and policies they have designed themselves will be implemented. If they are skeptical about their own ability to implement its own declared strategy, can you imagine how cynical the employees are?

Needless to say, few top managers convince their people that this is what they truly want. As a result, strategies remain unimplemented.

When helping companies develop new strategies, I frequently ask the planning team, when we are nearing completion, "How many of you think we *will* actually do what you have decided here, *will* run the company this way, and actually *will* implement these strategies?"

In a remarkably high proportion of cases, even the most senior vice-presidents and partners indicate that they do *not* think the new strategies and policies they have designed themselves will be implemented. If *they* are skeptical about their own ability to implement its own declared strategy, can you imagine how cynical the employees are?

CREATING A **NEW RELIGION**

It is incredibly hard even for sincere leaders to persuade their colleagues and subordinates that they have changed, and that they will manage to new standards.

People rarely accept that there has been a conversion on the road to Damascus. They never believe that there truly is a new religion in place. They always worry that their leaders will, when they are tested with a trade-off, go back to managing the way they did during the prior five, ten or fifteen years. Until they have hard evidence to the contrary, they don't think that *management* has the ability to say "no" to temptation.

When you think about it, this cynicism is understandable. Why should people think the leopard has changed its spots? If those closest to the leaders (the rest of top management) have a hard time believing that the leaders have truly changed their thinking, what hope is there for convincing the rest of the organization?

Managers must work constantly to act as a countervailing force against powerful financial reporting systems that almost inevitably fail to distinguish between *strategy* and *volume*: revenues and profits that are obtained by consistently with the strategy versus those that are obtained by compromising the standards implicit in the strategy.

The required changes fall into one of three categories: measures, behavior and personnel.

First, it is necessary to create new scorecards—built into the firm's regular reporting systems—that can distinguish between on-strategy work and off-strategy work.

> **Until they have hard evidence to the contrary, they don't think that management has the ability to say "no" to temptation.**

In one firm, as a piece of special analysis, it was discovered that 65 percent of its business came from only 100 of its total of 4,000 clients, and that most of the remainder were unprofitable.

The realization soon dawned that such periodic, retrospective analyses are not very effective. Once it accepted this, it was not too difficult to build this analysis into the firm's regular monitoring and managing approaches, making the firm's regular reviews of its results more "strategic."

Firms need to monitor which revenue streams are "building their assets" (helping them strategically) and which ones are "milking their assets" (good for the bottom line but not moving them forward). They could and should examine and regularly report such questions as:

- where do we get our business from? On-strategy sources or off-strategy sources?

- what percent of key targeted clients generate what percent of income?

- what percent of business in each year is from brand new clients and what percent is from clients (or types of work) that had been pre-designated as targets?

Next, a chief executive will need to ask what it is that he or she can do personally that will give dramatic evidence that top management is serious about adhering to the strategy in spite of short-term temptations. It is necessary for top management to *do* something (not just *say* something) that is both sufficiently dramatic and sufficiently different from the way that management has behaved in the past so

> A chief executive will need to ask what it is that he or she can do personally that will give dramatic evidence that top management is serious about adhering to the strategy in spite of short-term temptations.

that people in the organization start to discuss it and pass it on to others.

The challenge is figure out what the leadership could do that would be dramatic enough to indicate a break with the past, and would also be seen as credible and not just window-dressing. The answer will depend on the specific company situation, but I often suggest that leaders ask their people the question directly: "What could I do that would convince you that I am serious about sticking to our strategy and enforcing the standards that flow from it?"

Sadly, since people are always skeptical that specific individuals have changed, the most dramatic evidence that things have changed is when new people are put in key positions of influence. As one of my clients said, "The only way to *change* people is to change *people*!"

THE WISDOM OF THE ANCIENTS

In *The Wisdom of Confucius*, there appears the following exchange:

Zigong asked Confucius, "What would you say if all the people of a village like a person?" "That is not enough," replied Confucius.

"What would you say if all the people of the village dislike a person?" "That is not enough," replied Confucius.

"It is better when the good people of the village like him, and the bad people dislike him."

This ancient wisdom (Confucius died in 479 BC) summarizes what we have said in this article. You cannot and should not try to please everyone. Make sure that the right people like you, and it will be expected that others will not. That's how the world works.

> **Make sure that the right people like you, and it will be expected that others will not. That's how the world works.**

CHAPTER THREE

It's Not How Good You Are;
It's How Much You Want It

A critical aspect of strategy and its relation to the Fat Smoker metaphor is the need for individuals and organizations to resist short-term temptations and keep their actions focused on the strategic goals they have chosen for themselves. In this chapter, I explore the lessons that organizations can learn from what we experience as individuals by telling the story of my career, discussing what generalizations apply to other individuals, and then, finally, use those lessons to make some comments on firm strategies.

L ike many people, I had no idea what I wanted to do with my life when I left college. Armed with a degree in statistics, I took a job as a statistician. However, I soon discovered that it was neither my passion nor my area of special talent. Because I couldn't think of anything else to do, I went back to school for a master's degree, taking a teaching job to support myself.

Bingo! Without having planned it this way, I discovered that while my studies were a chore, I loved teaching and happily did that for a number of years. Of course, I was still teaching *statistics*, which did take the edge off my excitement a little.

I had no idea what opportunity was going to come next—I considered a lot of things, and waited,

In this chapter, I explore the lessons that organizations can learn from what we experience as individuals and use those lessons to make some comments on firm strategies.

eyes open. At one point I even applied to be a radio producer at the BBC (a job I didn't get).

My options expanded when my employer sent me as a delegate to a course Harvard Business School was running in Europe. I was suddenly presented with the huge, unanticipated opportunity to enroll in a doctoral degree course at HBS.

This was a big step, and one I was not sure I could pull off. Teaching in a local college is not the same as committing yourself to a career of producing original, scholarly research. I had never been top of my class in anything at any stage of my education (I still haven't been) but—well, it was worth a shot!

Another obstacle was that I had no money, so I would have to win one of the many generous scholarships offered in a variety of specialties. Two factors affected my choice. The first was my respect for a helpful, impressive faculty member. (Thanks, Jim Heskett!) The second was that his area also offered the largest scholarship.

That's how I ended up spending the next six years as a specialist in logistics and transportation. My doctoral dissertation was about grain transportation in Canada, and I ended up writing three books about the trucking industry and one about the airline industry. Given my focus today, people are always surprised to learn about that part of my history.

Which is, of course, the point! Did I know when I started whether transportation was going to be a fulfilling field for me? No, I didn't. Did I give it my full commitment and try to make it work for me? Absolutely. And when it became clear that it wasn't my life's calling, did I hunt around for the next chance to move on? You bet!

> **And when it became clear that it wasn't my life's calling, did I hunt around for the next chance to move on? You bet!**

It came with the chance to return to HBS three years after graduation, this time as a faculty member teaching management of service business and factory operations. (Yes, that was also a stretch, but you have to keep trying things, right?)

This leap of faith led to a new set of challenges. I already had a good job in a good university, with friendly colleagues. Giving that up to join HBS was equivalent to signing up for the Olympic team. With no guarantee that I could meet Harvard's standards and demands for faculty, I risked failure.

In spite of (or perhaps because of) the challenge, I took the new post. Eventually, at age thirty-five, after many unexpected twists and turns in my career since graduating from college fourteen years earlier, I finally started work on the topic that was to be my passion—professional services.

One more personal story before we search for the lessons: I always wanted to be a published author. Even in my college days, I thought how cool it would be to have someone who doesn't know you read your ideas and know your name.

There was only one problem: the act of writing has always terrified me! Whenever I have some writing to do, I get agitated, sweat, and avoid the task like the plague. In spite of this, my consulting career was launched (and is sustained) on writing.

In my academic career, I had written a lot of books and articles, but it was always under the threat of "publish or perish." I wrote because that's what academics are expected to do, even though the topics didn't always excite me.

My attitude toward writing began to change when I left academia to start my solo consulting business. I promised a magazine editor that I would write an article every month, knowing full well that I was committing myself to something that I would not necessarily enjoy, but that would get me where I wanted to go.

Having no choice, I lived up to my commitment and soon was being referred to as "that guy who keeps writing all those articles."

> **With no guarantee that I could meet Harvard's standards and demands for faculty, I risked failure.**

The articles weren't all good, and few people liked all of them, but my audience became accustomed to the idea that I was always going to be *trying* to communicate some fresh insight. The phone started to ring and my consulting career took off.

FORCE AND MOMENTUM

"Find your passion" is common career advice. But doing so can be a difficult process. You really need to work hard to find out what you can be passionate about. Unless you are very lucky, it can take many years to discover your long-term passions.

Successful people often appear to have had a rational career progression, with each step a seemingly sensible preparation for the next. The truth, however, is that most successful business careers have been based on experimentation and opportunism.

This is where business careers differ from careers in sports and the arts, for example. In those fields you usually have to choose an event or an instrument and dedicate yourself early and exclusively to that choice.

Business careers are not like that. Did Richard Branson know he was going to found an airline or a telephone company when he started selling records? Did Bill Gates ever know what products Microsoft was going to offer in a few years' time?

Like these (and other) successful businesspeople, you must be prepared to keep searching until you find out what truly excites you, even though you will be tempted along the way you to give up your search.

After all, what you are doing at any given moment is the result of a previous guess of yours as to what you thought would be fulfilling. So, your current situation is unlikely to be disastrous. It's probably "OK."

> **Most successful business careers have been based on experimentation and opportunism.**

This is where the world divides into two groups of people. One group will stroll down the path labeled "It's OK, so why change?" while another group will run down the path marked "It's only OK, let's find something better!"

My trainer once pointed out that to get the benefits of exercise you must use force, not momentum to develop a muscle. You don't develop a muscle by letting momentum move the equipment—it's the amount of force you apply that develops you.

The business equivalent is obvious. Career momentum can do a lot of the work for you and, indeed, carry you a long way. However, it is only when you add force to this that you create enhanced capability and extra achievement.

Actually, the conclusion is probably even stronger than that. Since even the most thrilling things become familiar after a while, passion and "engagement" will almost inevitably decline. There will be a life-long need to seek out new challenges. However, given the power of momentum, only those determined to get somewhere will actually do what it takes.

If you truly want to succeed (and many people do not want it badly enough to make it happen) then you must never settle, never give up, never coast, never just accept what is, even if you are currently performing at a high level.

If what you have now isn't what you dream (or dreamed) of, then you must keep looking, experimenting, and adapting. You must always search for the next thing you think you can feel passionate about, so that you will have a burning reason to show the discipline and drive that will distinguish you.

> **Career momentum can do a lot of the work for you and, indeed, carry you a long way. However, it is only when you add force to this that you create enhanced capability and extra achievement.**

Once you have found something to try, you must then throw yourself into it wholeheartedly and work at it with as much commitment as you can muster until you can answer three questions:

- Is this as exciting as I thought it was going to be?

- Is there a market for this? (Will anyone pay me to do it?)

- Can I make a contribution that others are not (yet) making?

For success to take place, all three must be answered affirmatively. If any component is missing you must move on.

Living your professional life this way is not easy. Each step in my career seems to other people like a terrific "step-up" accomplishment: giving up my statistics job to get a master's degree, signing up for a doctorate, joining the Harvard faculty, and then later leaving it to become a solo consultant.

The truth, however, is that for me and for most people each successive step was a terrifying leap into the unknown, requiring me to abandon the security of what I had without any certainty (or even probability) that it was going to work.

DETERMINATION

Sheer determination is the only explanation I can offer as to why I took these career risks. Determination drives people to risk failure. But taking those risks is the only path to achievement and success. Looking back, I am amazed at the chances I took, and am grateful that they worked out (though almost always with setbacks along the way). I often feel that my career has been one of "stumbling upwards."

You must always search for the next thing you think you can feel passionate about, so that you will have a burning reason to show the discipline and drive that will distinguish you.

There are no guarantees in life, and determination is only an essential ingredient, not a sufficient one. People try and some of them fail. But a lot more never try, and they cannot win.

The point is worth stressing. In a free market economy, scarcity (the relative supply and demand), not inherent value, is rewarded. If many other people have what you have, then you cannot earn a premium or distinguish yourself just because you have it.

Intelligence, IQ, brains, and smarts are all important, but they are also more common than drive and determination. The latter will be more highly rewarded and also more determinative of future success.

But you can't sustain lifelong drive and determination unless you are passionate about accomplishing something. Discipline for discipline's sake won't work.

The key lesson is that, for me and for others, lifelong drive and determination and the burning passion to get somewhere next, are the primary ingredients in personal (and organizational) success.

These principles also apply to most other walks of life. World-class athletes and artistic performers push themselves to the limit with repeated practice, training, and rehearsal. No matter how much natural talent they possess, it is their determination to do what it takes to succeed that makes them distinctive. The most talented performers must also practice the most.

Critical to success is the willingness to keep trying, always committing yourself to getting better, whenever you have just stumbled. This is hard. However, what may be even more critical is that successful people keep stretching when they are already doing well—which is even harder!

At any age—starting out or with retirement in view—the question that we must all address is: "Are we still trying to get somewhere? Do we have new worlds to conquer, and do we know what they are?"

As Napoleon said, "Glory may be fleeting, but obscurity is forever."

> **Lifelong drive and determination, the burning passion to get somewhere next, are the primary ingredients in personal (and organizational) success.**

BOUNCING BACK

Drifting along on momentum alone does not equip people with the energy, drive, and force needed to deal with the inevitable setbacks we all face: a missed promotion, ungrateful superiors and colleagues, or clients who fail to acknowledge a contribution.

Although it's tempting (and completely understandable) to tell ourselves: "Ah, I've been trying but the struggle is too frustrating. Why bother? Look what happens every time I try to change things" we must decide between withdrawing and renewing our efforts.

It's also tempting to beat yourself up. We have all lain awake at night thinking about mistakes we have made, things we could have done or said differently. Rather than rejoice in any accomplishments they have attained, people tend to dwell on missed opportunities and failures.

All of this is, of course, quite useless and unproductive. While we must avoid the extreme of always blaming external forces and other people for what happened to us, there is also no point getting stuck in a "doom loop" of self-criticism.

You're going to live with yourself for a long time. It's your own good opinion of yourself that matters more than anyone else's. Be kind to yourself. Plenty of people are prepared to judge you. Why do it for them?

The good news is that it's amazing how many times you can mess up in life and still succeed. As Winston Churchill reportedly said, "Success is the ability to move from failure to failure without loss of enthusiasm."

> As Winston Churchill reportedly said, "Success is the ability to move from failure to failure without loss of enthusiasm."

For example, George Washington barely won a battle in the early years of the Revolutionary War. His triumph was to prevail by *not losing* (and by inspiring others not to give up, despite terrible defeats and narrow escapes). Just staying in the game led to victory.

The key skill in life is not to never make a mistake! That's impossible. Rather, it is rebounding from (and fixing) your mistakes. Although it doesn't always feel like it, you can choose how you react to things that happen to you. You can let them get to you or you can brush them off. "OK. I blew it. Time to move on."

LESSONS FOR THE FIRM

If moods, emotional states, and characteristics such as determination and enthusiasm are the keys to individual success, what does all this mean for companies and firms?

The most important lesson is that, if they are to help their people and their organization overcome the Fat Smoker syndrome, then managers must, above all else, have the skills of being net *creators* of energy, passion, drive, and enthusiasm in other people.

Did Jack Welch or Steve Jobs (or anyone else) succeed mostly because they have higher IQ's than anyone else? They are certainly very smart people. But what made them special and successful was clearly something else: discipline, ambition, passion, entrepreneurship, energy, enthusiasm, engagement, and a whole host of closely allied characteristics.

What may be *more* important was the ability of these famous leaders to elicit (in different ways, perhaps) the same list of qualities (discipline, ambition, passion, entrepreneurship, energy, enthusiasm, and engagement) in the people and organizations they managed. If businesses are to overcome the Fat Smoker syndrome—succumbing to short-term temptations and gratification rather than implementing

> **Managers must, above all else, have the skills of being net creators of energy, passion, drive, and enthusiasm in other people.**

what they know is good for them—then the skill of managers in creating drive and determination will be a primary component in success.

Even Jack Welch, the recently retired chairman and CEO of General Electric, who had a reputation for being a hard-driving boss, wrote in his book **Winning**, "The job of any leader is to build self-confidence in the people around him. Make those people feel twelve feet tall. Clap for every achievement, no matter how small, with everybody around you. That's a hell of a lot more important than some finite strategy."

Unfortunately, too often, managers, rather than being creators of excitement, end up being net destroyers of it. Managers have been encouraged and trained to focus on tasks, activities, outcomes, and accomplishments, but they are rarely trained to understand and influence people's emotions, either as individuals or as groups.

For example, few business strategies are tested or chosen based on how motivating individuals and groups in the firm will find them. Product, service line, and location choices are still most frequently made on the detached, analytical grounds of "it's an attractive market."

Good corporate strategy is generally perceived as one that stresses analytics, planning, and logical, rational thinking. Managers are frequently skilled at figuring out what their firms should be doing. But they are less skilled at successfully motivating their people to accomplish these goals. Yet, as we saw in chapter 1, the primary outcome of strategic planning should not be analytical insight or smart choices, but a superior resolve to accomplish something.

> **Few business strategies are tested or chosen based on how motivating individuals and groups in the firm will find them. Choices are still made on the detached, analytical grounds.**

Too few organizations, and too few individuals, have implemented the basic insight that he or she wins who gets more done, and he or she gets more done who passionately wants to get to the next level of accomplishment. Creating and sustaining that ambition is management's *primary* task. It's obvious, but it's still scarce.

How well does your firm measure up to these behaviors and states of mind?

- New challenges are eagerly, continuously sought out.

- The firm and its people never rely on momentum for their success, but are always seeking to build new capabilities.

- Compared to key competitors, the people in the firm are distinguished by a superior, burning passion to get somewhere new.

- The firm emphasizes and requires adaptability, flexibility, and responsiveness as key virtues.

- The firm's strategies are created through continued and repeated experimentation.

- The firm is markedly superior in creating (not just hiring for) energy, excitement, enthusiasm, drive, determination, passion, and ambition.

- Service offerings, locations, and operating units are repeatedly assessed against these three key criteria: Do the people in the firm find this exciting? Are we making money? Are we doing something special that others are not doing?

- There is a restless refusal to accept "It's OK." People never settle, never give up, never coast.

> **Creating and sustaining ambition is management's primary task. It's obvious, but it's still scarce.**

- The firm sustains energy and investment actions both when things are going badly and when things are going relatively well.

- The firm does not judge its performance by the levels of its accomplishments, but by the "relative incline": whether or not it is improving relative to competitors on the characteristics it has chosen to compete on.

- Management is held accountable for its ability to create and sustain drive, enthusiasm, passion, ambition, commitment, and excitement in the individual members and groups that make up the organization. Managers who cannot do this are replaced.

Yes, these are tough standards. But if individual success is based on outperforming the determination of others, it surely follows that an organization that cannot create and sustain it must be in trouble, no matter how much organizational momentum it has.

LAST THOUGHTS

A final autobiographical note. In my mid-fifties, after having written a book per year for three years in a row, I suddenly found myself without energy. The lethargy lasted for more than two years, and I have never been so miserable in my entire life.

I discovered that I had sleep apnea, a medical condition that meant I hadn't had a good night's sleep in two years or more. There was (I understood only in retrospect) a reason that I had been physically and mentally exhausted. With treatment, my energy bounced back and I'm writing again. Great things are happening in my career, and I'm having a ball.

"I'm going to build a mountain / I'm going to build it high / I don't know how I'm going to do it / I only know I'm going to try."

As the Anthony Newley / Leslie Bricusse song goes: "I'm going to build a mountain / I'm going to build it high / I don't know how I'm going to do it / I only know I'm going to try."

CHAPTER 4

Are We In This Together?
The Preconditions for Strategy

If getting on (and sticking with) an ambitious program of self improvement is hard for an individual, the challenge for an organization is immensely greater. How certain is the organization that everyone involved is ready to go on the same journey together, making the same sacrifices to attain the same future goals? Especially in these days of mobility and talent shortages, where members of the organization at all levels must be treated essentially as volunteers, the first order of business in 'doing strategy' is confirming that people want to go somewhere together.

Managers build their plans and strategies on the assumption that people in their firm are ready and willing to be team players, acting collectively to create or achieve something in the future.

The truth, however, is that these attitudes cannot be assumed to exist. In fact, they're notably scarce. In many firms—perhaps even most—these preconditions for strategy may not exist.

It is hard to identify and create buy-in for what "we" (i.e., the firm) should do if there is no strong sense of "we"—a mutual commitment and sense of group loyalty and cohesiveness. Similarly, talk of new initiatives can be meaningless if the members of the firm are not committed to embark on a journey together into the future.

> **It is hard to identify and create buy-in for what "we" (i.e., the firm) should do if there is no strong sense of "we".**

This was brought home to me when I was facilitating a strategy discussion in an industry that has a long tradition of hiring, celebrating, and rewarding stars—individualistic, solo operators. As we discussed the investments and initiatives necessary to implement the strategy identified by management, one of the "players" in the room asked, "Why would I want to do this. What's in it for me?"

It must be immediately recognized that having this thought is normal. The industry I was working with is only unusual in the (refreshing?) willingness of people in this business to actually say things like this out loud. In other industries and professions, they just think it all the time, without actually saying it!

As we worked through the issues, it became increasingly clear that there were major differences among the people in the room, the key players in the company, whose participation and collaboration would be essential to pull off *any* strategy. The issue was not the specifics of the proposed strategy. What came through clearly was that no commitment to each other—or to their joint future—existed.

In this situation and on other occasions when I have explored this, it has become clear that people differ on their desire to be engaged in a joint, mutually-dependent enterprise (collaboration) and the time frame they wanted to apply to their decision-making (future-orientation). These differences are either inherent personality characteristics, or at least strongly-held preferences.

> **People differ on their desire to be engaged in a joint, mutually-dependent enterprise (collaboration) and the time frame they wanted to apply to their decision-making (future-orientation).**

Some prefer working as part of a team, with joint accountabilities, responsibilities, and rewards. They want to be part of something. Others, however, freely admit that they are most comfortable (and seek out) situations where they can be independent—judged on their own individual merits and accomplishments, without being tied to the performance of others.

The other major difference between people is their time frame. Some people have an appetite for high-investment, future-oriented strategies. They are willing to defer (if necessary) some immediate gratification in order to invest—to get the chance to reap higher rewards in the future. Others are reluctant to invest, even in their own future. They prefer to focus on "winning today," letting tomorrow take care of itself.

Combining these two dimensions leads to the identification of four kinds of preferences that individuals (and companies) have:

- Type 1 is the solo operator who values independence and wants to make little investment in the future, but is willing to bet on his (or her) ability to catch fresh meat each and every day. I call this the Mountain Lion approach. "Pay me for the meat I bring back today (or this year)."

- Type 2 is the individual who prefers to act in coordination with others, but doesn't like to invest (or defer gratification) too much. I call these people (collectively) the Wolf Pack. "If we act together we can kill bigger animals, but I'd better eat well too or I'm joining another pack!"

Types 1 and 2 may be unwilling to invest or "bet on the future" for a variety of reasons, including risk aversion.

- Type 3 is the individual who wants to be independent, but is interested in building for the future by investing time and resources to get

> Some people have an appetite for high-investment, future-oriented strategies. They are willing to defer (if necessary). Others are reluctant to invest, even in their own future.

somewhere new. I call such people Spiders, who patiently weave their web to catch more flies in the future, or Beavers, who build dams to provide a home for their (own) family.

- Type 4 is the individual who wants to be part of something bigger than he (or she) can accomplish alone, and who has the patience, ambition, and will to help the collective organization invest in that future. I call this group the Human Race, since one of the things that differentiates *Homo sapiens* (at least in scale) from other species is the ability to act collectively to build and develop a civilization.

Note, however, that Type 4 could also be termed an Ant Community or Beehive, where individuals slave for the benefit of the community, suppressing and subsuming their own identity within the whole. (This interpretation is most likely to be applied, naturally, by those who do not place themselves in this category).

	Capture Rewards for Short-Term Performance	Build for the Future
Interdependent Team Players	Wolf Pack	Humans (or Beehive)
Independent Solos	Mountain Lions	Spiders / Beavers

I don't have a precise metric to measure the differing orientations described here, but I have found two proxy questions to be useful.

On the issue of independence versus team play, I ask people whether, in general, they would prefer rewards in their organization to be based (compared to the current arrangements) a little more on individual performance or a little more on joint rewards for joint performance. I then ask if people would like their firm to invest more, compared to the current arrangements, in its future, even if this meant that they as individuals would have to accept less current income in the form of salaries and current bonuses.

These two (imprecise) questions tend to cause people to reflect on their true preferences. The underlying issue is not really about pay schemes, but phrasing the questions this way tends to crystallize the issues for many people.

I ask people in the group to indicate (anonymously, if possible) which of these four preferences best describes their own personal preferences, and where they would put their colleagues. (At this point you may wish to pause and guess what percent of all your colleagues would place themselves, by preference, in each category).

In the particular company where I first explored the model, all four groups were well represented, although only 10–20 percent put themselves in the "I want to be part of something bigger than me that is working to build for the future."

Thirty to forty percent put themselves in the "solo short-term" (Mountain Lion) category, with approximately twenty to thirty percent each in the "team-play short term" (Wolf Pack) and "solo builder" (Beaver) categories.

I don't know if the fact that only 10–20 percent of key players wanting to be "team-play builders" strikes you as low or matches your experience, but it leads to an interesting question:

> **What do you think the chances are of melding people who describe themselves mostly as short-term solo operators into an institution that has a differentiated reputation?**

What do you think the chances are of melding people who describe *themselves* mostly as short-term solo operators into an institution that has a differentiated reputation?

My own conclusion, then and now, is clear. An organization that has these proportions might succeed through individual, entrepreneurial activities, but it would be quite literally incapable of having a company strategy. For example, no common reputation or differentiation could be achieved in the competition either for clients or talent. Firm leaders who tried to develop and implement company strategies would be wasting their time.

Using this model in numerous firms has revealed diversity among people who had previously thought of themselves as loyal members of their firm. They may indeed be loyal, but their desires and preferences differ so much on the key dimensions that, in many cases, no strategy can accommodate the diversity of preferences among the members of the group. Although a prevalence of those choosing the "team-play building" preference is not necessary, when a majority of the key people really *don't* want to act collectively in building for the future, it is meaningless to develop plans as if they did.

The mixture of preferences may place very severe limits on what an organization can achieve. While there may be some logic and merit in *like-minded* people banding together (whether they be Mountain Lions, Wolves, Spiders/Beavers, or Humans), an organization made up of an unmanaged mix of such types is unlikely to function well.

The preconditions for strategy are rarely exposed and examined, possibly because the implications of discovering a disparity of preferences can be very scary and disruptive.

A significant degree of agreement is a requisite for successful implementation of any strategy. This agreement is quite scarce.

Very few people or organizations have frank and open discussions about this surprising revelation.

The preconditions for strategy are rarely exposed and examined, possibly because the implications of discovering a disparity of preferences can be very scary and disruptive.

A group of people who all identify themselves as preferring to operate as "independent short-term" players can succeed in many businesses. (See, for example, the discussion of "Hunters and Farmers" in my book *Managing the Professional Service Firm*). Many businesses can be, and are, constructed around "star players" rewarded for their short-term results.

Similarly, a Wolf Pack can achieve something that is called "strategy" and can align its recruiting, systems, and rewards around a strategy of collaborative short-term actions, if that's what everyone wants.

However, without a majority of key players committed to collaboration and investment in the future, it is unlikely that most of what is usually considered to be firm-level strategy can really be accomplished. Before discussing their plans, firms need to discover whether their people really want to go on a journey—any journey—together.

DEALING WITH **DIVERSITY**

If you were to conduct this poll in your organization (asking people either to place themselves in one of the four categories, or to estimate what percentage of their colleagues they would place in each group), what choices would you have if you found that you had a broad diversity of preferences?

Option One: Try to Accommodate Differences

Is it possible to find different roles for people, so that individualists and short-term players can be accommodated by playing specific

> Without a majority of key players committed to collaboration and investment in the future, it is unlikely that most of what is usually considered to be firm-level strategy can really be accomplished.

roles in the organization without compromising the commitment and determination of the majority? This option would clearly be very desirable if it were practical. It would require the least disruption to the status quo.

Manufacturing corporations have different activities (such as sales, production, or finance) that may require different attributes, so could other organizations, such as professional service firms, also accommodate different orientations?

I believe that idea *may* work, but not by allowing people of different orientations to play the same role in the organization. There may be differences between the desirable characteristics of those in sales and those in production, but I doubt that much variety can be acceptable *within* one of these groups.

If one sales person (or team) is taking a collaborative building approach, is it acceptable for another to act in an independent, short-term fashion? (If the answer is yes, it would be hard to see what is meant by saying the organization has a strategy!)

The only way different species can live together peacefully in the real world is if they do not compete for the same resources.

That means the Wolf Pack *should be* a completely separate department (preferably in a separate building) than the Mountain Lions, who have their own "deal" (privileges, responsibilities, and metrics). It is necessary to keep one group away from the others if they are to coexist!

Is it possible to articulate to people that the team approach is in their individual best interest? Is it possible to persuade people that relying on and working with others will enable them to achieve their personal goals?

> **The only way different species can live together peacefully in the real world is if they do not compete for the same resources.**

Personally, I'm not sure I have much hope in this area. Is it really possible to get short-term individualists to "do the right thing" for the company's long-term best interests through persuasion or systems? Can they realistically set individual goals that further corporate goals?

I am increasingly skeptical that this traditional "managerial systems" approach can be made to work. In my experience, it falls apart when we try to create an amalgam of many types of workers, and then pretend that everyone is measured and rewarded on the same things, that everyone has the same performance standards, and that everyone plays the same role.

Ultimately, it's too much to ask that excessive biodiversity be accommodated. I doubt that you can have a random, equal mixture of all types and make it work well.

Option Two: Work to Change People's Orientation

The second choice for dealing with biodiversity is to try to affect people's orientations. One way to possibly accomplish this is to craft a sufficiently compelling vision for the future that even those who do not start off with an initial preference for team play or investment are willing to sign on.

The potential success of this option depends on one critical question. Are people's orientations relatively fixed, based on underlying personalities and preferences? Can they change with time or become dependent upon specific circumstances?

The answer is important. If people's orientation toward teamwork and time-horizon is context specific (i.e., dependent upon the particular team and strategies being proposed), then there is hope that some process of building commitment to a strategy can successfully forge collective action even from those initially unwilling.

Are people's orientations relatively fixed, based on underlying personalities and preferences? Can they change with time or become dependent upon specific circumstances?

If, however, there is a relatively sizable fixed component in people's attitudes, then no strategic planning process can be successful. The choice will either be to abandon strategy or to separate from those who do not wish to enter upon the journey together.

My own hypothesis is that the fixed component in many people's personalities is relatively high. People really do differ on to how they want to live their lives. Solo operators rarely develop a preference for team play, and people who want immediate gratification rarely develop the patience to sacrifice even a portion of today for an uncertain future—especially if they have to make that investment in conjunction with (and be dependent upon) others.

In this view, it is not the clarity or the glamour of the vision that affects people's lack of buy-in to collective, future-oriented strategy, but people's willingness to participate in strategy at all.

Another hypothesis that emerges from this is that it will be hard, if not impossible, to reconcile differences through pay schemes: It will be difficult to change working behaviors based on deep personal preferences, even through the clever construction of incentives.

If this hypothesis is correct, people who do not conform to the basic orientation of the company should either be in or out of your organization, depending upon what that organization wants to accomplish. Companies, according to this point of view, must achieve a consistent, careful philosophy about the kind of people they bring in, and the kind of people they keep. (See chapter 15 on "The One-Firm Firm.")

It is not easy, but it can be done. In spite of what I have argued above, the relatively "fixed" component of people's collaborative and future orientation is not completely determinative. It is very encouraging, I have found, to discover how many people will, in fact, choose to accept

> **Solo operators rarely develop a preference for team play, and people who want immediate gratification rarely develop patience.**

a well-articulated philosophy, even if it is not the one they might have chosen for themselves.

If the firm is prepared to bring the issues of collaboration and future orientation to the surface, and (through some open process) ask participants to commit themselves explicitly to a joint, building future, then significant degrees of buy-in can be obtained.

Options Three and Four: Split Up or Cover Up

The consensus-building approach does not always work. Sometimes, a firm which has been in existence for a long time can find it impossible to define a coherent strategy because there is no consensus on why the relevant people are together. Other than, of course, historical accident and mindless accretion, which is how many businesses seem to have grown.

In a world in which many organizations have been put together with mergers, acquisitions, and extensive use of lateral hires, the underlying problem may grow in importance, rather than diminish.

In such a situation (which is remarkably common) there are really only two options: splitting up and issue avoidance.

Splitting up is not necessarily a tragedy. If the people in an organization truly want to pursue different objectives and operate in different ways, it can be better for all concerned to confront the topic and, amicably, go separate ways than to squabble or silently resent each other!

Specifically, if people truly differ in their orientations and objectives, it may become necessary to ask those who are not prepared to commit collaboratively to leave the organization.

> **Specifically, if people truly differ in their orientations and objectives, it may become necessary to ask those who are not prepared to commit collaboratively to leave the organization.**

This sounds tough, brutal, scary, and risky, and it is all of those things. Notice that the argument is *not* that doing this is unconditionally necessary. Rather, the argument is that it must be done if an organization is going to be capable of having a strategy—any strategy.

The fourth alternative is by far the most common: avoidance of the issue, papering over the differences, ignoring the problem, or (worse and most common) complaining all the time that everybody wants different things and nothing gets done.

Issue-avoidance is, of course, the way fat smokers would deal with the problems!

It is commonly observed that the biggest problem with developing strategy is implementation. It may be the case that the problem is more profound, that the members of the organization have insufficient commitment to each other—or their mutual future—to implement *any* strategy.

CHAPTER FIVE

What's **Our Deal?**

In the previous chapter, we discussed the need to ensure that the members of an organization are prepared to act together to pursue a joint (or at least common) goal. In this chapter we explore how an organization can and should go about deciding what its members are agreeing to. If strategy is (at least in part) about deciding which diet and exercise program to live by, then on what (and how) does an organization need to achieve consensus?

At a conference, I heard a number of successful firm leaders describe how their firms had achieved significant growth and profitability. A common phrase used by each and every one of these firm leaders was "making sure that all the key people were 'on the same page.'"

Clearly, it was important that something was agreed to and shared among the members of these firms. But what? What does "being on the same page" really mean? And how is it done?

A HIERARCHY OF CONCEPTS

A common collection of integrating concepts could include these choices, in what some people would describe as descending order of importance:

What does "being on the same page" really mean?

- Purpose / Mission

- Vision / Direction

- Values / Principles

- Culture / Rules of Behavior

An organization that begins with an agreed-upon *purpose* (or *mission*) should be able to communicate credibly, both externally and internally—WHY it is in existence.

This allows the organization to communicate more easily a *vision* of its future, and hence its *objectives* and *direction*—WHAT it is trying to achieve.

It can then derive a set of *values* or *principles* that the firm is going to operate by—HOW it plans to operate in order to achieve the purpose, the vision and the objectives.

The set of values and principles will then define the firm's *culture* and hence its *rules of behavior*. This is more HOW—the way things are done around here.

This ordering of concepts is just one approach. Notice that it leaves out the word "strategy" and makes no reference to specific objectives or targets.

Unfortunately, in practice, these various integrating concepts rarely achieve what is hoped for when they are developed, and many people have become (appropriately?) cynical about these concepts.

Many more firms have "mission statements" than actually have missions, and it is the rare organization where everyone believes that the officially declared statement of values is strictly adhered to.

For example, many more firms have "mission statements" than actually have missions, and it is the rare organization where everyone believes that the officially declared statement of values is strictly adhered to.

Have all of these concepts lost their practical value? Should firms and their leaders still take the time to attempt to build consensus around things like purpose, mission, vision and values? If so, how can it be done in a way that actually has a practical, real-world impact? Where do you begin?

Tempting as it might be, it would be a mistake to abandon *all* uses of these terms. Some mixture of these things is almost certainly needed:

- To create a sense of common, joint enterprise

- To define the organization

- To set its boundaries

- To give it a direction

- To mobilize the organization's members

If you were a real-world chief executive trying to lead your organization, where would *you* begin to grapple with these concepts?

STARTING WITH PURPOSE

Among others, Nikos Mourkogiannis stresses the importance of beginning with "purpose" in his book ***Purpose: The Starting Point of Great Companies.***

Howard Schultz, CEO of Starbucks, has been quoted as saying that "People want to be part of something larger than themselves. They want to be part of something they're really proud of, that they'll fight for, sacrifice for, trust."

Where a clear, believable, palpable purpose exists for the organization, where its reason for existence and what it is trying to achieve is clear, a multitude of business virtues follow almost automatically. Among them are the following:

- Decision-making can be made easier (at all levels) by considering whether or not

Have all of these concepts lost their practical value?

decisions advance or inhibit the organization's purpose. Things will happen more smoothly and more efficiently, with fewer false starts.

- The organization can attract energetic, committed employees who believe in and share the purpose and, equally beneficial, scare away people who don't want to participate in that purpose.

- Less heavy-handed oversight and management will be required to keep things on track, since everyone will be using the same principles to guide their interactions and decision making.

Notice what the proponents of "purpose" are saying. The argument is that by (credibly) eliciting commitment to a "cause" *other* than maximizing shareholder value, shareholder value (and other measures of financial performance) will actually increase, not decrease, because people will contribute their extra efforts and dedication.

Purely financial purposes, the argument goes, will fail to elicit this extra energy. "Work hard to maximize the owners' profitability!" is not much of a rallying cry if you are not an owner. It may not even be that effective among the partners themselves in a large partnership, for example, if there are hundreds or thousands of them scattered over many distinct departments, service lines, cities, countries, and continents.

It's also worth stressing that the practical test of whether having a declared purpose (or mission) helps your organization achieve greater things is not whether the marketplace believes what you claim to stand for. Rather, it is whether or not the people inside the organization truly believe that all decisions are

> **"Work hard to maximize the owners' profitability!" is not much of a rallying cry if you are not an owner.**

actually made (or should be made) on the basis of that purpose or mission.

Only if *they* believe that the purpose or mission is real will you actually elicit the extra levels of energy, commitment, collaboration, dedication, and long-term thinking that will produce the superior results.

This is, of course, a researchable, testable proposition. You could survey all of your people, right now, and ask them how well they think your organization is living up to its purpose, mission, vision or values. If they say it is, there's a high probability that you are already reaping the commercial benefits. If they say it is not (or if you're not sure you want ask or disclose the findings) you have to question whether, in purely practical terms, you have learned how to make purpose, mission, vision or values work for you.

Achieving a functioning purpose is hard. It is not only a problem of management actually possessing an "ideology" and having the discipline to always act in accordance with it. It requires that the organization attracts only those who are prepared to help pursue the organization's purpose without substituting their own agenda.

As discussed in chapter 4 ("Are We in This Together?") not all people are predisposed to enjoy mutually dependent activities designed to build for the future. Mr. Schultz of Starbucks may be right about most people being eager to seek out a cause, but not all people.

I'm not saying building a common purpose cannot happen, or that it's not immensely powerful where it does exist. I'm merely reporting that it's incredibly scarce. There are relatively few organizations that credibly convince their people that management

Few organizations credibly convince their people that management won't take advantage of short-term "off-purpose" opportunities to advance net shareholder value.

won't take advantage of short-term "off-purpose" opportunities to advance net shareholder value.

Contrary to what many leaders seem to believe, there's no point in declaring that your organization has purpose or mission if your people don't think you will stick to it unwaveringly. You'll just destroy your credibility.

As an employee at one of my client organizations said recently, "Inconsistency is very demoralizing." Not to mention confusing and unproductive. You cannot get your people to dedicate themselves to a cause you stick to only occasionally. As one chief executive said, "You can be certain that, as night follows day, any ambiguity will be construed against you."

And you cannot build an organization committed to a purpose, mission, vision, or values if you hire otherwise exceptional people who are not susceptible to such appeals and do not share a dedication to achieving them.

BUILDING **COMMITMENT**

So, if you think that your organization does not (yet) have an energizing, motivating purpose, should you take your people through some kind of process to see if they are willing to sign up for one?

Maybe. But let's be practical about what would be required. Whether you are talking about purpose, mission, vision, values, goals, objectives or almost ANY of the traditional concepts that people use, the only practical way to make them real is to do two (simultaneous) things:

1. Stop talking about the future destination, and start thinking about the *rules* you would have to live by in order to get there.

Inconsistency is very demoralizing.

2. Translate the generalities of the *organization's* purpose, mission, values or principles into what it

would mean for *individuals* and confirm that the organization's members are, in fact, prepared to be held accountable and live by those individual rules.

As the Fat Smoker metaphor is meant to indicate: declaring that you "want to get fit" doesn't really indicate that you have chosen anything. It certainly doesn't, by itself, persuade the listener that you are committed to that goal.

However, if you stop talking in the language of *destinations* (goals, targets, purposes, missions and aspirations,) and instead discuss whether you are prepared to accept strictly observed operating *rules* like "I will exercise for 30 minutes five times a week and eat no more than 1,500 calories per day" then your commitment shows. Now it becomes exponentially more likely that you will achieve the goal.

We all know that, as a practical matter, it is insufficient to say "We will *try* to exercise for thirty minutes five times a week and eat no more than 1,500 calories per day." In both personal and business life, you know that the minute you allow ambiguity or uncertainty (i.e. loopholes and exceptions) into a statement, people will become less certain about what you will actually do as a leader, what they are buying into and what they are required to do.

So, to discover if your firm is willing to pursue a particular purpose, mission, vision or values, you must discuss these questions:

- Are people willing to have all decisions, large and small, judged in accordance with that purpose?

- Are they willing to be personally and individually accountable for progress toward that purpose, mission, vision, value, or principle?

Stop talking in the language of destinations and instead discuss whether you are prepared to accept strictly observed operating rules.

Imagine, for example, a group of firm leaders sitting around discussing their firm's future. Imagine that someone proposes that the firm should commit itself to the purpose or mission of being "the leading firm" in its area.

What might this mean in practical terms? Does this mean that everyone agrees that the firm should only do high-end work and turn away work if it does not command premium fees? If not, what is the rule going to be?

Does it mean, as an example, that the firm will only work for chief executives and no one else in the client organization? Does it mean that the firm will only employ those who are truly superior and will ask the merely competent to leave? If it means *none* of these things, then what, if anything, would it mean to be a "leading firm"?

As a means of discussing people's understanding and commitment to what is being proposed, notice that propositions become more clear if they are phrased in the negative.

To say "we want to be the leading experts" is not the same thing as saying, for example, "We will not stay in a business that we cannot charge a premium for." Usually, saying what you will *not* do communicates more than what you say you will do.

If you cannot articulate a set of *binding* rules that people will agree to be governed by, then you probably do not have a purpose, mission, vision or values.

As always, this is meant to be a pragmatic point, not a moral or aesthetic one. It used to be said that your culture was what people did when no one was looking. That's not a bad way of summarizing all this.

You don't have a purpose or mission (or a set of values) when you declare them. You have them when you put in place "consequences for non-compliance".

If the people in the organization share (and *use*) a common set of decision-rules whenever they are faced with choices, the likelihood that you have an integrated firm with a common purpose, mission, vision or values is high. If they don't (or won't) accept the same (clear, unambiguous) decision-rules, then you may have a successful firm, but it's not clear that all parts of your firm will be on the same page.

You don't have a purpose or mission (or a set of values) when you declare them. You have them when you put in place "consequences for non-compliance"—processes that *respond* to each and every instance when the organization (or individual) fails to adhere to the purpose, the mission, the values or the culture.

STRATEGY AS JOURNEY, NOT DESTINATION

What all this reveals is that "doing strategy" is not really about selecting objectives, targets or future states. ("We aim to be the best!") That's too imprecise, and too easy to honor with lip-service.

It *doesn't matter* whether you choose to start by discussing purpose, mission, values or culture (or anything else). The rules you choose to live by determine your future, not the targets you aim at.

Start by asking yourselves, what are we prepared to be uncompromising about? This will tell the world (inside and outside the organization) who you are, what you are, and what your vision, mission, purpose and values are.

Political science and history teach us that you can determine the very nature of a society by agreeing upon its constitution: establishing the core, inviolable principles and regulations as to how decisions will be made.

By concretely stating the rules that govern decision-making and, equally important, the rights and obligations of citizens in the community, the very identity

> **What are we prepared to be uncompromising about? This will tell the world (inside and outside the organization) who you are, what you are, and what your vision, mission, purpose and values are.**

and character and its future potential of the society can be determined.

So it is with business organizations. When "doing strategy," it can be difficult, if not impossible, for firm leaders to say definitively what businesses the organization will get into, what services it will offer and in what parts of the globe it will offer its services.

In fact, making and declaring choices in these areas can be politically risky if they do not include, as priority targets, areas of the business that the organization is already in. No one wants to be identified as being in an "off-priority" part of the business.

However, if firm leaders can propose and build support for, the decision-making processes and rules (i.e. the constitution) that the firm will follow in all of its decisions, then something both meaningful and powerful can be created.

Another insight into this was provided by Cristian Mitreanu in a fascinating article called "Is Strategy a Bad Word?" He wrote:

"What explains the relative failure of most organizations to create effective strategy? Part of the problem… can be traced to their interpretation of the word strategy itself… In war, objectives can often be clearly defined, and so strategy is thought of as a means to a specific end… By contrast, goal orientation becomes arguably inappropriate when success has to be indefinitely sustained."

I call this "acting as if there is no final whistle." It means running the organization not to attain particular targets in a particular time frame, but recognizing that, one way or another, the organization will continue into the indefinite future.

It's rather like thinking of an organization as a biological entity or a species. It's not in the

"Acting as if there is no final whistle."

choice of *objectives* that a species differentiates and sustains itself, but through its special ways of adapting and responding to shifts in its environment.

Consider also the well-known computer simulation that, by specifying, in advance, some basic parameters (including the rules of reproduction) shows the emergence and struggle of species. Wonderful patterns emerge, and some species flourish while others die out.

The differences between these "species" are not differences in objectives, targets, purpose or mission. The differences that really determine the future are the rules they employ to make their decisions when faced with choices.

In game theory (a branch of mathematics about decision making) the term "strategy" doesn't refer to any particular decision, or group of decisions. Rather, strategy is a set of rules or guidelines that tell you how to go about making decisions. Defined that way, it closely correlates to the concepts of values, ideology and principles embedded in the way the organization makes its decisions.

Where clear, unambiguous decision-making rules exist, there is the opportunity for a clear rallying cry for people either to buy into or to leave, and it makes delegation of decision-making upwards, downwards and sideways a lot easier. Everyone knows the REAL rules.

PARTICIPATION

Even if an organization *thinks* it has a clear, unequivocal agreement on purpose, mission, vision and values, it is nevertheless should periodically revisit its values and trace through what rights and obligations they imply for individuals, top to bottom.

An organization's "rules of engagement" have a tendency over time to be taken for granted over time. They can fall into neglect not through malice but

Strategy is a set of rules or guidelines that tell you how to go about making decisions.

by being taken for granted. The slow accretion of small decisions and actions, none of them actually seriously wrong, can
nevertheless cause an organization to eventually operate in ways
contrary to its declared core beliefs, principles and rules.

There is tremendous power in giving people the opportunity to discuss whether they still wish to be governed by the
rules that have defined the organization in the past. There is
also great power in asking people to affirm (or re-affirm) their
"pledge of allegiance" to those rules.

People are more likely to live in accordance with the rules
for mutual accountability, mutual contribution, and shared
values that they have helped to shape. (See my coauthored book,
First Among Equals.)

It is a common tendency to draw up a set of values or principles (or, as I prefer, decision-rules) and present them simultaneously to all of the key players at some annual meeting or
specially convened strategic planning meeting or retreat.

I believe that this is a mistake. As noted above, an organization may be made worse, not better, by pretending to advocate a set of standards it is not actually prepared to live by.
And everyone in the organization will be looking "upwards" to
see if "those guys" are truly serious before they commit themselves to the cause.

Accordingly, the best way to approach this re-evaluation is to
begin with a very small inner circle of top management leaders,
who can look each other in the eyes and ask: "Are these really
the decision-rules we as leaders
are prepared to stick with? If we
advocate them, will our people
believe that we will keep the faith
to adhere to these strategies?"

Only when management at that
level becomes committed will it
be time to slowly proceed to the

> **People are more likely
> to live in accordance
> with the rules for mutual
> accountability, mutual
> contribution and shared
> values that they have
> helped to shape.**

next level, making the case as to why the organization should live by the decision-rules, and building the necessary consensus and buy-in.

The top level's commitment will filter down throughout the organization, to the junior levels, and finally to the outside world. It can't be done effectively in any other way.

DECISION-MAKING RULES

So what might be some possible decision-making, constitution-forming rules?

Here are some suggestions for firms to consider:

- We will make all decisions based on putting the clients' interest first, the firm's second and the individual's last. We do not accept people who fail to operate in this way.

- We will achieve levels of client satisfaction that result in client referrals becoming our main source of new business.

- We will have no room for individualists—those who put their personal agenda ahead of the interests of their team.

- We will design reward systems to reflect a judgmental assessment of overall contribution to the success of the firm, not just short-term individual performance.

- We will require, not just encourage, everyone to learn and develop new skills. The organization accepts its obligation to help each individual achieve this.

> **The best way to approach this re-evaluation is to begin with a very small inner circle of top management leaders, who can look each other in the eyes and ask: "Are these really the decision-rules we as leaders are prepared to stick with?**

- We will invest a significant amount of time each year in things that will pay off in the future.

- We will select, evaluate and remunerate those in managerial roles based primarily on the success of their group, rather than on their individual performance.

- We will, individually and collectively, operate with a "stewardship" mentality toward our junior people, accepting the obligation to coach, mentor and develop those who report to us.

- We will not tolerate abuse of power or position, a lack of respect in dealing with other people at any level in the firm, politicking, individuals who cannot be relied upon to keep their word, or shirking or dumping of responsibility. Only those of the highest honor and integrity will be allowed to retain membership in the firm.

These are, of course, only *possible* decision-making rules. They are not necessarily the best (although a case can be made for their effectiveness in creating organizational success) and they are not the *only* choices a firm could make. Each organization will achieve better clarity and effectiveness by establishing its own nonnegotiable decision-making rules it is prepared to live by. (See, however, the discussion of the "One-Firm Firms" in chapter 15.)

Once the decision-making rules are in place, it should be easier to trace through the "rights and obligations" that members of the organization have: what they agree to sign up for when they join, what they agree to be held accountable for, and what they can reliably expect from the organization (and other individuals in the organization).

> **Once the decision-making rules are in place, it should be easier to trace through the "rights and obligations" that members of the organization have.**

My recommendation is not to accept the rules offered here. Rather, it is to figure out which rules you, your management and *all* your people would be prepared to accept and never compromise. When you are done, you will know your purpose, your mission, your values and your strategy.

PART TWO:
CLIENT RELATIONSHIPS

The Fat Smoker syndrome—that we know what to do, but find it hard to be patient enough to do the things that will lead us to our goals—finds no better illustration than in the area of client relations.

One of the most common and ambiguous terms in business today is "client-centricity" or "client focus." Many businesses claim to have it. But if the essence of a relationship is a willingness to earn and deserve what you want by first focusing on the other party in the relationship, few companies really are client-centric.

Many firm's so-called "client relationship plans" are not really plans to build a relationship at all. They are *sales* plans, which is not the same thing. A sales plan is a set of activities designed to *get*—to generate revenues in the short run. A relationship plan is a set of activities to *give*—doing things that will build an asset—the relationship—that will continue to generate revenues into the future.

Charles Green, author of *Trust-Based Selling*, has a wonderful analogy. He points out that many companies have the client focus of a vulture—they pay close attention to what the clients are up to, but only in order to figure out the right time to pounce. They are focused on the benefits they can get from the relationship, not on how they can provide greater benefits *to* the client. Like all aspects of the Fat Smoker syndrome, people are constantly looking for the "magic pill" that will bring them the benefits of a long-range program, without actually having to do the work.

In the first two chapters, we contrast the difference between marketing aimed at short-term success and that aimed at building long-term relationships. In the last chapter in this section, we explore the tensions between the noble aspirations of firms and the way they actually manage their marketing efforts.

CHAPTER SIX

Do You Really
Want Relationships?

The process of building relationships is similar to the self-improvement strategies we have already discussed in previous chapters. They require investment today in order to get (greater) benefits tomorrow. As I discuss in this chapter, many individuals and organizations may say they want relationships, but lack the willingness to do what it takes to earn them.

I n *The Trusted Advisor*, my coauthors and I pointed out that building trusted relationships with clients leads to many benefits: less fee resistance, more future work, more referrals to new clients, and more effective and harmonious work relationships with the clients.

However, many people have built their past success on having a *transactional* view of their clients, not a *relationship* one, and it is not clear that they really want to change. Stated bluntly, people may say that they want the benefits of romance, yet they still act in ways that suggest that they are really interested in a one-night stand. As with all aspects of the Fat Smoker syndrome, the desire for instant

People may say that they want the benefits of romance, yet they still act in ways that suggest that they are really interested in a one-night stand.

gratification can prevent us from doing what is best for us in the long run.

In romance, both sides work at building a mutually supportive, mutually beneficial relationship. They work hard to create a sense of togetherness, a feeling of "us."

Each side tries to truly listen to what the other is saying and feeling. The emphasis in discussions is less on the immediate topic at hand, and more about preserving the emotional bond and the mutual commitment.

Rather than seeking immediate short-term gratification and reward, romance relies on making investments in the relationship in order to obtain long-term, future benefits.

This romantic scenario is seemingly attractive, but when you look at the way most professionals deal with their clients, and how many clients deal with their professional providers, there's very little of it to be found.

Most professional-to-client interactions involve little if any commitment to each other beyond the current deal. The prevailing principle is "buyer beware." Mutual guardedness and suspicion exist, and the interaction is full of negotiation, bargaining, and adversarial activity. Both sides focus on the terms, conditions, and costs of temporary contact. It's "*us* versus *them*" throughout the encounter.

This is the way many professionals and their clients want it to be. They *want* a transaction, and may not yet (if ever) be ready for a bond. Rather than acting to build relationships, both sides might initially have the brakes on.

> **Rather than seeking immediate short-term gratification and reward, romance relies on making investments in the relationship in order to obtain long-term, future benefits.**

After all, relationships require making a commitment and incurring obligations. They also mean focusing and being selective: You can't chase after every opportunity if you want to build relationships. To be good at relationships, you must have patience and know how to trust others.

Moving from a one-night-stand (transactional) mentality to a romance (relationship) mindset does not depend on incremental actions, but requires a complete reversal of attitudes and behaviors. One approach is not necessarily "better" than another, but there is a real choice to be made.

EXPERT **VERSUS ADVISOR**

Although it is not an identical comparison, the difference between transactions and relationships is similar to the distinction between being an expert to one's client and being an advisor.

An expert's job is to be right—to solve the client's problems through the application of technical and professional skill. In order to do this, the expert takes responsibility for the work away from the client and acts as if he or she is "in charge" until the project is done.

The advisor behaves differently. Rather than being in the right, the advisor's job is to be helpful, and to provide guidance, input, and counseling to the client's own thought and decision-making processes. The client retains control and responsibility at all times; the advisor's role is subordinate to this, not that of a prime mover.

Viewed this way, it is easy to see why many professionals, while they may pretend to the virtues of being an advisor, actually do not want to be one. They do not want to advise; they want to take charge.

The asset manager does not want merely to recommend investments to the client; he or she wants to control the client's funds. The trial litigator, similarly, does not want to provide input on trial strategy. He or she

> An expert's job is to be right, the advisor's job is to be helpful.

wants the client to cede authority to the warrior to do battle as she or he sees fit.

Naturally, there is nothing wrong with either role. There are many times when the client is best served by selecting the true expert and putting his or her affairs in their hands. On other occasions, the client may truly want and need an advisor.

The only mistake, on either side, is to pretend. A practitioner who is wedded to expert ways ("Leave this to me, I'll get you the result you want") has every right to practice that way. He or she has no right to complain if some (or many) clients prefer a different approach.

Of course, it would be foolish for someone who really prefers being an expert to pretend that he or she is an advisor. The mentality is different. The personality required is different. The skills required are different. The work experience and the fulfillments are different.

An expert who wants to be an expert is going to be miserably poor at pretending to be an advisor, and is going to resent the client throughout the entire project (which apparently happens a lot)!

MANAGING AS A RELATIONSHIP OR AS A TRANSACTION

The issue of choosing between transactional and relationship approaches exists not only in dealings with clients but also in dealings with people inside the firm.

When I conduct seminars and workshops on managerial topics, those who pose questions often want to know how to get *other* people (partners, subordinates, employees) to change their behavior.

"Are you saying," they ask me, "that I need to show an interest in my subordinates as people and care about their career ambitions?"

The questions they ask nearly always suggest a transactional viewpoint, with the implication that we are just fine; *they* need to change. When I suggest solutions based on building relationships with these other people, my questioners are often frustrated.

"Are you saying," they ask me, "that I need to show an interest in my subordinates as people and care about their career ambitions?"

"Only if you want them to respond to you," I reply. "If your subordinates feel that you are prepared to work at a relationship with them, ensuring that both sides benefit, then they will give you more of what you want. That's human nature, not a political or religious point.

"But if they think that you, their superior, are just trying to get out of the deal more of what you want from them—harder work, more billable hours, whatever—then they will respond in kind. They will view you as you are viewing them —useful only to the extent that they can get out of it what they want in the short run.

"There will be no long-term loyalty and no commitment to the larger interests of the firm, because *you* have set the pattern that this is truly a temporary transaction, not a relationship. If you treat people as objects, tools or as 'others,' they, in turn, will treat you instrumentally. It's completely predictable and unavoidable."

This analysis is not always received well. Managers are always trying to get more from that amorphous group of *them* (the subordinates) without having to build personal relationships. The reasons are often the same as in the client situation. Developing relationships means creating commitments and obligations that people do not want to incur.

In spite of what they say their goals are, many individuals are just not prepared to do what relationships require—in *any* context.

> **Managers are always trying to get more from that amorphous group of them (the subordinates) without having to build personal relationships.**

Their resistance reveals not only their attitudes toward clients, but also their attitudes toward people in general. It is their attitudes that must change, not just their daily habits.

THE ATTRACTIONS OF TRANSACTIONS

We must be wary of romanticizing romance (or the advisory role). Relationships are not the best answer for all people at all times. There are also benefits to both parties in transactions.

Relationships can be scary, particularly if the parties rush too quickly into creating obligations that neither side is yet ready to accept. Both client and provider may be reluctant to commit until they have developed significant experience with each other. Growing relationships is very personal and intimate. You actually have to be interested in others, listen to what they say and care about, and pay attention to their moods and needs.

Few of these skills are required in a transaction. Where they are required, they are only needed for a short period of time, usually during the initial seduction (i.e., negotiating the deal) when people play games pretending to care about each other.

After that, the transactional approach (focus on the getting the job done, not on the other person) allows you to remain detached and unengaged, which is very attractive to some people. You can emphasize the technical skills for which you trained, and not be stressed by the need for interpersonal, psychological, emotional, or political nuances. For many professionals, this is a great blessing.

Relationships, by their very nature, are not as clear-cut as the negotiated contract terms of a transaction. On both commercial and psychological grounds, it is easy to see why some individuals may prefer the clarity (and short-term gratification) of a "propose, get hired, deliver, get paid" transaction.

Transactions are also very appealing to those who find comfort in the rational, the logical, or the analytical approach.

Transaction skills are very "scalable": Expertise at winning and delivering transactions can be codified and disseminated quickly across an organization. It is less clear that the interpersonal skill of relationship building can be developed as quickly in a business that wants to grow rapidly.

Transactions are also very appealing to those who find comfort in the rational, the logical, or the analytical approach—a description that includes many people who chose professional and technical careers. Little in professional training prepares you for the psychological complexities of dealing with or liking clients.

The table on the next page shows some of the differences between transactions and relationships:

Additional differences exist between the two approaches. In pursuing a one-night stand, a small degree of exaggeration, misrepresentation, and manufactured appearance is normal and even expected. Perhaps people rarely lie, but they rarely tell the whole truth either.

For example, clients hide their projects' true objectives and budgets for fear of giving too much away and being at a disadvantage in the negotiations. Or providers try to create the appearance of greater experience, competence, and capabilities than they truly have.

A trusting relationship, however, requires complete integrity. Telling your spouse even a small lie will destroy years of relationship building.

Switching from a transactional to a relationship approach to business requires a revolution of attitudes and behaviors. Gradual change will not take hold, because everything people have learned through their successes in transactions may work against them in learning how to be good at relationships. The most successful Don Juans and Donna Juanitas are unlikely to make the best spouses.

> **The most successful Don Juans and Donna Juanitas are unlikely to make the best spouses.**

Transactions	Relationships
One-night stand	Romance
Them	Us
Opponents	On the same side
Short-term benefit	Long-term benefit
Suspicion	Trust
Goal is to make yourself look attractive	Goal is to understand the other party
Negotiate and bargain	Give and be helpful
Preserve options, avoid obligations	Make a commitment
Focus on the present	Focus on the future
Develop a detailed contract	Be comfortable with ambiguous understandings about future reciprocity
Main goal is to prevail	Main goal is to preserve the relationship
Style can be impersonal, detached	Style must be personal, engaged, intimate
Preparation and rehearsal of what we're going to say and do	Adaptability and flexibility to the responses of the other party
Listen to what they're saying	Listen to what they're feeling, why they're saying it
Usual feeling during the interaction is tense, enervated	Usual feeling is relaxed, comfortable
Interactive style is defensive, protective	Interactive style is open, inquisitive

WHICH APPROACH **DO PEOPLE WANT?**

What percentage of clients seek relationship advisors rather than transactional experts? What percentages of providers would rather be relationship advisors than transactional experts? I don't have hard data on this point, but I regularly poll my seminar audiences about what they look for when *they* are trying to buy professional services.

Fully eighty percent of the typical audience reports that they would prefer to hire a true advisor and, if they could find someone skilled in taking that approach, would be willing to pay a premium for it. Twenty percent would not, preferring to seek out either the best technical expert or the low-cost provider.

When I ask the same audience which approach they and their firms are currently taking, the numbers are reversed. Eighty percent report that they mostly market themselves as experts (or are currently perceived as such), although many have dreams of changing this and becoming a "trusted advisor firm."

These results are not, of course, scientific. But the difference between what people say when they are buyers and what they say when they are providers is striking.

THE CLIENT **AS ENEMY**

Although viewing dealings with clients or employees as a transaction is normal (and may be the most common form of interaction), there is a danger that continuing to view clients as "*them*" can degenerate into perceiving the client as the *enemy*. This can breed reactions that spiral into self-defeating behavior for both parties involved.

> **Eighty percent of the typical audience reports that they would prefer to hire a true advisor and, if they could find someone skilled in taking that approach, would be willing to pay a premium for it.**

All too often, the client becomes a competitor for things the professional wants (money, challenge, or control), not a partner in obtaining them.

All this can lead to behavior that worsens the situation. Professionals act in ways that are pompous, patronizing, condescending, or arrogant, and the clients react to them by being (in turn) defensive, more guarded, and even less "relational." Things begin to spiral downward.

As Charles Green points out in his book, *Trust-Based Selling*, you can tell that a professional provider is treating the client as the enemy when he or she prefers to work back at the office rather than at the client's location. Each side, jealous and insecure about its control, competes for power over the agenda or the outcome of a meeting or phone call. Unlike healthy relationships, which expose and deal with problematic issues early, transaction players develop an inability to confront the other side on difficult issues.

As a result of all this, when client and provider become opponents, exaggeration, misrepresentation, selective disclosure of key information, and careful management of appearances become common on both sides. Both sides fight to be right and to prevail, rather than to collaborate on finding a solution.

This impasse thwarts the best interests of all parties concerned. By treating providers with suspicion, buyers create an atmosphere that makes providers more reluctant to show a sincere interest in any client need or requirement beyond the terms of the contract.

> **When client and provider become opponents, exaggeration, misrepresentation, selective disclosure of key information, and careful management of appearances become common on both sides.**

In turn, this unresponsive behavior reinforces the buyer's perception that providers are not worthy of trust and must be kept at arm's length, watched like a hawk in case they take advantage of the client.

Like some ancient rivalry, or a bad marriage, the origins of the dispute are lost in the mists of time. It is impossible to discover who was first responsible for treating the other badly.

All that can be observed now is a set of resentments and accusations of being treated poorly by the other side. Each side can point to specific behaviors that show that *they* (the other side) are unfair, unreasonable, and untrustworthy. Each side has concrete evidence of behavior by *them* that proves that "we are justified" in our thinking poorly about *them*.

As a result, clients become more demanding and controlling in their buying behavior, and providers become more insincere and less responsive in their dealings with clients. Both sides end up actively encouraging the adverse reactions from *them* that they are trying to avoid.

Other examples of dysfunctional "client as enemy" behaviors include:

- Rehearsing what you are going to say to the client in proposals and presentations rather than how you plan to get a true conversation going

- Avoiding conversations with clients because you want either to remain in control or avoid having to treat the client as a person

- Avoiding contact with clients unless there is something concrete to talk about

- Trying to sell more work to get what you want rather than what the client wants

- Requiring that all agreements and decisions be documented and formally approved, rather than trusting each other's word

By treating providers with suspicion, buyers create an atmosphere that makes providers more reluctant to show sincere interest.

The most important agenda for most professionals is to ensure that they do not allow their transaction business to spin out of control into "client as enemy" behavior. Among all the outcomes, this is the worst, with no winners.

Transactions are inevitable. Clients increasingly treat professionals as vendors. They audit bills, use purchasing departments and consultants in their selection processes, bargain hard, and emphasize contractual terms. Once this has begun to happen, it is clear that the client organization has categorized you as the "evil other" what will follow, with immensely high probability, is going to be a transaction.

But a transaction is not necessarily a tragedy. As long as enmity does not build up, this approach can achieve great success. Once you are working with the client on the transaction, you have the opportunity to then take advantage of the client contact to build a relationship for the next time.

However, firms must be vigilant in identifying where they are engaging in "client as enemy" activities, and discuss ways to eliminate them. In addition, they must identify and eliminate anything they may be doing that causes the clients to view the firm as the enemy.

As Patrick McKenna, my coauthor on *First Among Equals*, observes, "The first tangible acknowledgment that many clients get from their professional service provider is a standard retainer agreement that lays out in no uncertain terms 'what we are going to do for you—and to you—if you don't pay our bill in a timely fashion.'"

> Once you are working with the client on the transaction, you have the opportunity to then take advantage of the client contact to build a relationship for the next time.

"How's that for a terrible way to start?" Patrick asks. "Why not make sure that the firm's first communication with the client is a letter of thanks for having been chosen, providing a note of reassurance to the client that he or she has chosen someone with some human sensitivity?"

If relationships are not always possible, the very least a firm can do is to ensure that it handles its transactions professionally, and does not play the transaction game in such a way as to alienate the very clients it seeks to win and serve.

MAKING THE **TRANSITION TO ROMANCE**

Many people believe that individuals, by the time they reach positions of influence in their careers, cannot readily change. They also believe that if firms want to build relationships, they must recruit, develop, and retain people who have a predisposition for romance. They do not try to change transactional people in the middle of their careers.

There is a great deal of truth to this observation. In *Managing the Professional Service Firm*, I wrote about two types of firms: *hunters* (based on opportunistic individualism) and *farmers* (based on collaborative teamwork). Many firms have tried to make the transition from the former to the latter, only to discover that it is extremely difficult to turn individualists into team players.

The few institutions that have succeeded in this transition have done so not by changing people, but by replacing them. Firms began to change only when the collaborative team players achieved positions of power and could insist on their approach.

Another approach to making changes of this kind is to complement "old-style" players with people who have the "new" attitudes and skills. Firms pair technical experts with "client-friendly" salespeople, encouraging them to meld skills and work together to win and serve clients.

The real challenge, however, is for all of us as individuals, not as firms. Transactions are common because they involve less hard work and demand fewer skills.

> **Transactions are common because they involve less hard work and demand fewer skills.**

They are yet another example of the Fat Smoker syndrome: doing what is better for us in the long run is the less frequently chosen path. We would rather do what gets us through today than invest in our future.

Ultimately, however, mutual trust will allow both sides to get more of what they seek. Relationships are not more "noble" than transactions, but where they can be created they are much more profitable.

Many professionals will want to make the terrifying and difficult transition from skilled seducers to relationship-minded collaborators. Clients *can* be successfully led into a mutually supportive relationship and away from treating us with suspicion, but only if we throw away the bad habits of viewing them as "*them*", and throw ourselves wholeheartedly into developing the new skills of relationships.

The key first step is to recognize that romance and relationships work by *earning* and *deserving* what you want to get back from the other party. Whenever a trade-off occurs, the rules of romance require that, instead of acting defensively to protect your own interests, you put the client's interest first and keep the faith that this relationship-building act will be repaid through future reciprocity. As **The Trusted Advisor** tried to show, this is not idealism since it leads to higher returns, but it does require an act of faith.

Accordingly, the course of wisdom for newcomers to the approach is to be highly selective in choosing a first relationship to experiment with. As in all change efforts, a small-scale first experiment that has a high chance of yielding an early success is the wisest approach. Don't begin with your most important clients. If you are going to learn a new skill, it is better

> We must have the courage and patience to shake off old ways of viewing other people and become willing to learn new ways of dealing with them.

to do so in a situation where any initial fumbles will not be costly.

If they are to capture market premiums, providers cannot, in the long run, afford to have clients continue to view them as the adversary. Providers need clients (and employees) to think of each encounter as an opportunity to build teamwork and a collaborative relationship. We must each decide whether, if we truly want the benefits of romance, we have the courage and patience to shake off old ways of viewing other people and become willing to learn new ways of dealing with them.

CHAPTER SEVEN

The Friendship Strategy

Many firms claim that what distinguishes their organization is that their people are client-centric and act like trusted advisors. However, few of these organizations, when they hire, have programs to select for these attitudes and skills and few have systematic programs to help their people develop them.

An organization where everybody did have a consistently high level of friendship skills would truly achieve a differentiated strategy! This chapter uses the lessons of our personal lives to explore how the habits and skills of friendliness can be applied in a business setting.

I n trying to understand how to build business relationships, we should draw upon what we already know from relationships in our personal lives. People often don't do this. It sometimes seems as if, when they come to work, people leave behind everything they have learned about interacting effectively with others.

If you have an active social circle and people like being with you, the odds are that you will have a significant advantage in learning the skills and habits of business development. If, on the other hand, you're a social recluse, you will find it more difficult to convince clients to see you as a trusted advisor they wish to work with.

The way most clients choose professionals is essentially identical to the way people choose their

When they come to work, people leave behind everything they have learned about interacting effectively with others.

friends. They look for professionals who can (a) put them at ease, (b) make them feel comfortable sharing their fears and concerns, (c) inspire trust in their ability to oversee both the client and his transaction, and (d) prove their dependability.

Creating these feelings in others begins with having the correct attitude—a sincere interest in others. However, the outward signs of this genuine caring are often conversational and interpersonal skills.

If you want to win a client's business, it's necessary to give the client the chance to talk to you, person to person, about *their* needs, wishes, and wants. The key is to make it easy and comfortable for the client to share his or her feelings and secrets. In short, if you really want to win a client's business, you must know how to have a *conversation*.

There's nothing conceptual or special in this use of the term "conversation." Think of it literally, the way we all use the word in everyday speech. The characteristics of a conversation include:

- It's person to person; not role to role. People use normal language, not "corporate-speak."

- Both sides talk, and what one says is dependent upon what the other has just said.

- Both parties are engaged in joint problem solving; neither is trying to win or prevail.

- It's designed to allow people with different views to learn from one another.

Marketing (and/or selling) begins to work when a conversation moves away from being a role-to-role exchange of capabilities, contracts, and costs and becomes a person-to-person interactive dialogue about ideas, beliefs, and

> **If you really want to win a client's business, you must know how to have a conversation.**

perspectives. Only then can it build the chemistry, confidence, and commitment that lead to new revenues.

Imagine a dinner party conversation. What makes a good conversationalist in such a setting? He or she:

- Has a fresh point of view, but does not try to thrust it upon everyone else

- Speaks politely and respectfully

- Tells good stories to illustrate key points

- Is good at drawing other people's views out and drawing them into the conversation

- Speaks intelligently on a variety of subjects, but is not afraid to admit areas of ignorance

- Avoids trotting out well-worn arguments or clichés.

- Listens with genuine interest

- Is light-hearted in style, but always respectful of others' views

All of these conversational skills also apply to effective marketing and selling. You may remember to behave this way at a dinner party, but do your client meetings really meet these criteria? What about your seminars, speeches, articles, blogs, and websites?

Is the tone of your client interactions friendly, inviting the client to chat, to think about ideas and to encourage both sides to get to know each other as people?

This doesn't always come naturally to everyone. For example, if I am in the wrong mood and find a dinner party to be an effort, I may ask the person on my left, "And what are your hobbies?"

> **Conversational skills apply to effective marketing and selling. You may remember to behave this way at a dinner party, but do your client meetings really meet these criteria?**

"Oh," the person might reply, "I love mountain climbing."

At this point I have to fight an overwhelming desire to turn immediately to the person on my right side to save me from having to ask the first person a follow-up question. Mountain climbing! Ye gads, this is going to be a long night!

Other people, however, can and do immediately think of three or four follow-up questions—Where do you go? Do you climb alone? What got you started in this?—and can continue posing additional questions all evening long.

By the end of dinner, their table companion, who has done nothing but talk about herself the whole time, has come to regard the questioner as an enjoyable person to be around. She will look forward to meeting again.

So it is with business development and client relations. The most trusted advisors in every profession are not those who have a ready answer for every client problem, but those who can, through questions and conversational style, put the other person at ease, make him want to tell you about himself, and engage in a dialogue.

And, just as in personal life, this is done not by trying to be impressive, but by learning how to show a genuine interest in other people and keep them talking.

> The most trusted advisors in every profession are not those who have a ready answer for every client problem, but those who can, through questions and conversational style, put the other person at ease, make him want to tell you about himself, and engage in a dialogue.

Can this habit be abused? Yes. Will it work if you are only faking it? No. Can you leave it out? No.

Doing this requires that you are comfortable in your own skin, and that you are who you are. Much of traditional marketing is designed so that people *aren't* required to put their own humanity on display. They hide behind formal, corporate language and tactics.

Not only are such approaches ineffective, but they create the impression that the professional or the individual (and the firm) is afraid to let its hair down. (For a deeper exploration of how the conversation metaphor can be put to work, see "Marketing is a Conversation", a coauthored article on my website).

LEARNING TO **MAKE FRIENDS**

I had to learn many lessons about friendship and client relations the hard way. For years, I have worked for clients who have been gracious enough to invite me to dinner the evening before or after my work with them. They weren't trying to get more work out of me; they just wanted to be sociable.

However, I have resisted being "on duty" after a long day's work. It's not that I don't like my clients, but that I prefer to unwind by being alone. I'm not *that* sociable by nature. (I don't drink. I don't like sports. I like the Bee Gees. You get the idea.)

I now regret this aversion to socializing. No matter how successfully I may have built relationships by focusing on my clients during the workday, I have missed many additional opportunities to build profitable and fulfilling long-term client relationships.

A TALENT **FOR FRIENDSHIP**

Some people do have a talent for friendship. My late and much lamented friend Roger Bennett was so good at friendship that, in his forties, he still kept in regular touch with people he went to school with at age twelve, and with people from all walks of life and of differing tastes, social standing, income levels, and preferences.

Much of traditional marketing is designed so that people aren't required to put their own humanity on display. They hide behind formal, corporate language and tactics.

Roger could talk sports with some people, switch to an intellectual discussion of philosophy with others, and share cooking tips with a third group. Lots of people considered Roger their best friend, and few people did not enjoy his company.

Yet he was never anything but himself. He was not a chameleon, acting differently just to blend in. He fit in everywhere because he was interested in a broad range of things.

To paraphrase actress Angelina Jolie, who was asked in a television interview if she had to like the characters she was portraying in order to depict them well, "You can't love everything about everyone. But there must be something there. The key is to find that one small slice of overlap between you and them, and focus on that overlap, ignoring everything else."

I don't know about acting, but that sounds to me like a perfect recipe for human relationships.

Friendships can be based on finding even a single mutual interest, no matter how small. If someone else has to mirror you to be "your kind of person," you will have few friends.

Surprisingly, it also turns out that you are more likely to build a bond with someone by letting him help you than by being too eager to help him. My wife Kathy is involved in a variety of handcraft groups. She reports that some of her most dedicated friendships began when she confessed her (relative) weaknesses and accepted help from others, whereas those she helped often resented having to seek out or accept her input.

Again, this principle applies to client relationships and business development. You will accomplish more by saying to potential clients, "I'm not sure I understand why you are doing things the way you do; could you explain it to me?" than you will by saying, "If you'll just shut up and listen, I'll tell you the right answer to your problem."

> **The key is to find that one small slice of overlap between you and them, and focus on that overlap, ignoring everything else.**

As professionals, we sometimes incorrectly think that to be impressive, we must demonstrate our competence by never revealing our weaknesses or areas of ignorance. One of the ways you build friendships is to let people help you. Developing the self-control to do it that way is a lifelong learning process!

START AS YOU **MEAN TO BEGIN**

When I was young I thought that the way to make friends was to become an interesting person. Eventually I learned the truth: You don't make people want to spend time with you because they feel good about *you*. You do it by making them feel good about *themselves* when they are with you.

Ask yourself: Do people feel comfortable around you? (No, she's always trying to be the center of attention.) Do they enjoy themselves when they are with you? (No, he's always trying to win arguments and prevail.) Do they feel that they can let their guard down and tell you how they really feel and what they are really worried about? (No, because when I do, she's always trying to take advantage of me. I don't trust her to be really interested in me.)

None of this means you need to make people feel good by engaging in false flattery, which is soon detected and rejected. It means that you learn to talk and act in ways that make people feel comfortable and safe around you. They feel that you are *on their side*. Then you can disagree and have lively debates without taking things personally, because the friendship matters more than anything else.

The same is true in business development. The key to getting hired is not convincing clients of things about you ("I'm terrific, trust me!") but convincing them that you will look after them.

> You don't make people want to spend time with you because they feel good about you. You do it by making them feel good about themselves when they are with you.

It's also worth pointing out that, with people, you get points for trying. It's like a romantic relationship. You don't have to be perfect. Your partner just wants to see that you're sincerely trying to do the right thing. Your motives are more important than your abilities.

FRIENDSHIP **ATTITUDES AND BEHAVIORS**

Abilities, however, do count, and that's where getting started early matters.

Suppose you want to be good at building romance: getting another person to work with you to build a mutually beneficial, mutually supportive relationship. What characteristics would make you good at this? Most of us have discovered that whether it is love, friendship, or work, people respond best when they believe that you are (among other things) *considerate, supportive, understanding, and thoughtful*.

The answer is likely to be some variant of the Fat Smoker syndrome. You know what's good for you, but it takes attention to a lot of detail today to get the reputation that's going to benefit you in the future.

Some Friendship Attitudes
Appreciative
Considerate
Dependable
Empathetic
Respectful
Responsive
Sensitive
Supportive
Sympathetic
Understanding

A reputation for being supportive, for instance, must be earned through social habits. And to be seen as considerate, you have to be able to remember information that people share about their lives, proving that you listened and paid attention. It also helps to follow up with skillfully phrased questions about what you were told last time you met. The idea is demonstrate concern, not intrusiveness, with a question like, "How did it work out with that guy you met?"

Another thoughtful, classic business gesture is to email someone something you found on the internet that relates to that person's interests. To achieve the desired effect, this must not be just a formulaic, phony, overused gesture, but a genuine, useful overture. With practice, you can learn to tailor language and small courtesies to the individual recipient.

Other social graces work in both personal and business life. It is remarkably effective to remember to telephone your host or hostess the day or week after a party to say something like, "I just wanted to say thank you for the party the other night. I had a great time. What time did you eventually get to bed after cleaning up the mess we all made?"

Exactly how formally or informally this will be expressed is different in different parts of the world and among different types of people, but the habit of expressing appreciation (and judging just how much is enough without being false) can—and must be—developed over a lifetime.

Similarly, it is quite powerful to call clients after a business meeting to say something such as, "I just wanted to let you know how much I appreciate the opportunity to work with you. Thanks! See you next time, as planned."

Done with sensitivity to local culture and phraseology, such a call can go a long way toward making the other person realize that you do not just see her as a

Do people think I am considerate, supportive, understanding and thoughtful?

"business contact," but as a person with whom you want a friendly relationship. Not everyone will reciprocate, but the majority of people will.

If you do not develop the habit early in life, the act of making such a telephone call after a meeting could feel awkward, eliminating the casual, comfortable "just a quick call between us friends" atmosphere that you wish to create.

For example, my friend Roger worked hard at staying in touch with everyone. He didn't need an excuse to telephone, but would just pick up the phone to ask clients and friends how everything was going. For him, one context was no more difficult or embarrassing than the other. It was just the way he dealt with people.

To be viewed by other people as *supportive* also takes thought and careful attention to language. It is important to remember that friends don't judge each other. They don't evaluate. They don't point out each other's weaknesses. Even when asked directly, "Do I look fat in this?" friends work hard to find the language that doesn't disparage, with a reply like, "I like the other dress better."

Suppose that your friend has a child who is badly behaved. You don't say, "Your kid is a little horror!" or "You're raising that kid incorrectly," even though both statements may be true. Instead, a friend could say something like, "Have you ever thought about doing or saying such and such to little Ashley?"

Having the ability to respond with the right phrase in real time takes practice, as do all social skills. Can you recall how difficult it was to find the right words and tone when you first wanted to signal to someone that you were interested in a date? Can you imagine what it would be like if you were restricted to those same methods today?

> To be viewed by other people as supportive also takes thought and careful attention to language. It is important to remember that friends don't judge each other.

So it is with business development. If urgency to win business motivates you to contact a potential client, then you will be under too much pressure to instantly develop these relational skills. Better to start practicing early, when there is less pressure for immediate results and more room to develop your own style and to discover what works for you.

People who are good at friendship work hard at developing joint habits and routines, whether it's as simple as discussing last night's sports game or going to the same place each time for a cup of coffee. For my friend Roger and me, regular sessions of playing cribbage became our way of cementing and celebrating our bond. I rarely played the game with anyone else.

Good friends go out of their way to celebrate each other's small triumphs, and make it their business to be there in times of their friends' need. They stay alert for any opportunity to help, in ways big or small, without keeping track of who has done how much for whom. That's *exactly* what happens in effective business development.

INVESTING **IN FRIENDSHIPS**

If your reaction to spending your time on these things is that doing so will not pay off for you immediately and therefore is not worth doing now, then you are missing the whole point about human relationships. You are going to be very bad at convincing people to entrust you with their business.

If you only do things when they benefit you in the short term, your attitude will be transparent. People will see that you view them "instrumentally," interested in them only to the extent that you can get what you want. And if they detect this in you, people will be less apt to give you what you want.

The key to business development success is making people

Having the ability to respond with the right phrase in real time takes practice, as do all social skills.

believe that you are truly interested in a two-way relationship, and that you are willing to earn and deserve your relationship. You must first make deposits in the "trusting relationship bank" if you wish to make withdrawals later.

You need to become interested in people and to initiate relationships, and that means being willing to ask someone out for a drink without being self-conscious about it. And the only way to get to that stage is to have a history of doing it!

Along with interest in others, one of the most important habits of friendship is taking the initiative and doing the inviting, not just waiting to be invited. It's the old "if you want friends, be a friend" you remember from childhood. The way you get people to ask you out is to ask them out first. If it feels like an uncomfortable, courageous act the first time, well, it is.

We all need to reach the stage at which we can talk to someone we're interested in (a client or a romantic prospect) without being frozen into inaction by our hopes and fears. The guidelines are well known. Keep it casual, keep it small, and take it a step at a time, but get out there and start meeting people.

Yes, we hated it when our parents told us to do that as children. It's no less terrifying today, but it works.

Go ahead! Ask people about their work lives and their personal lives. Do it as an exercise in developing your "curiosity muscles." Do it as an exercise in asking good follow-up questions about what people tell you. Do it to develop your ability to understand other people who are not like you. Do it now.

> **If you only do things when they benefit you in the short term, your attitude will be transparent. And if they detect this in you, people will be less apt to give you what you want.**

As individuals, or as organizations, it is possible to set out to develop friendship skills. However, like all aspects of the Fat Smoker syndrome, it requires a concerted effort to invest today in building skills (and relationships) that will pay off tomorrow. Unless they are already naturals, relatively few individuals—and even fewer organizations—have the self-discipline to stick with the program. That's why it's a successful strategy for those who do.

CHAPTER EIGHT

Doing It **for the Money**

Marketing discussions within many organizations deal in a detached, un-emotional way with market segments, unique selling propositions, cross-selling opportunities, and a whole host of subjects other than whether people feel that they are interested and trying to help those they are try-ing to serve.

However, If you, the provider, are acting in such a way that I can see that you are primarily trying to serve yourselves—get my work and my money—and only coincidentally or secondarily trying to help me, then the odds go down that you will win my work.

The basis for all successful marketing, selling, client service, relationship management and cross-selling will be the provider's success in convinc-ing me, the buyer, that you are truly interested in me and are truly trying to help. But, in spite of what firms say about their mission, vision and val-ues, that's not how many firms manage their marketing efforts.

I t was one of those familiar conversations that I often have:

"We want to get more of our people involved in busi-ness development."

"Is this a new idea, or have you been working at it for a while?"

"Oh, we've been working at it a lot. We've tried quite a few things."

"Such as?"

"Well, the first thing we did was try to convince them of the wonderful things business development would do for the firm if we were all successful at it."

"And?"

"They all agreed, but only a few were moved to action by things that were good for the firm. Most of the others were more interested in things that were good for them personally.

"So what did you try next?"

"We tried to make it personal. We changed our compensation system to put more reward in for business getters."

"Did that work?"

"A little, but it mostly just ended up paying more to the people who were already good at it. It turned out that promising to pay you if you got terrific at a completely new skill wasn't enough to overcome the lack of confidence that many had about whether they *could* learn it."

"What happened next?"

"Well, we tried using the pay scheme again. We started rumors that we would cut the pay of or fire people who couldn't generate business."

"And how well did that work?"

"Well, it generated a lot of fear, but even fear and terror didn't turn non-marketers into marketers. We ended up spending more time fighting about the new reward system and even less time discussing new marketing ideas. It seems as if the minute you discuss money, people can't think about anything else."

"Interesting. What did you try next?"

"Well, we put all our people through sales training courses."

"Were they effective?"

"They were very useful for those who were already interested in business development. They didn't have much impact on those who weren't interested. It was pretty much a waste of time, because it was the ones who weren't interested that we were trying to reach."

> **"We want to get more of our people involved in business development."**
> **"Is this a new idea, or have you been working at it for a while?"**
> **"Oh, we've been working at it a lot."**

"Anything else?"

"Oh, yes. We designed a process for targeting our key clients with cross-discipline teams and we gave people access to marketing staff specialists, laying out a program of how to make relationship building programs effective."

"And what happened?"

"Well, where individual people or groups did what we planned, it worked fabulously. Some people always wanted to do this in an organized fashion. But many of our supposed teams never did execute the programs they had themselves submitted as plans."

"Why not?"

"The same syndrome, I suppose. Tools, systems and organization are wonderful aids for people who already want to do this stuff, but they seem to have little impact on people who don't want to. If the underlying problem is attitude, no amount of processes, forms and support is going to change things."

"So?"

"Well, what do you think we ought to try next, David? What's the latest thinking?"

FIRST, STOP DOING **WHAT DOESN'T WORK**

Notice the amazing range of things that firms have tried to get people involved in business development. Included in the preceding dialogue are references to:

- Visions
- Rewards
- Punishments
- Training
- Processes

> **Tools, systems and organization are wonderful aids for people who already want to do this stuff, but they seem to have little impact on people who don't want to.**

- Support resources

- Restructuring of teams

And, I'm told, they haven't worked as well as people hoped they would. They don't seem to elicit *enthusiastic* participation in business-getting.

It's probably no coincidence that, with the possible exception of providing a "vision," all of these approaches resemble the efforts of a fat smoker to try quick fixes to obtain short-term payoffs.

Firms do not address the central question that non-participants have: "*Why* should I get involved in all this?" They fail to give people a credible or effective *reason to get involved.*

Firms keep trying to prove to people why their efforts would be good for the firm ("Do it for the glory of the institution; do it to achieve our strategic goals") or because it will make them rich ("Don't worry about whether this is interesting stuff—do it for the money!") Typically, this motivation is accomplished simply by announcing that those who bring in business will be rewarded. And that's it! They just say, "Do it and we'll pay you!"

Not only are these appeals not always effective but, perhaps surprisingly, encouraging professionals to put effort into business development primarily for the money turns out to backfire badly. Frequently, *less* money is earned, not more.

WHAT'S WRONG WITH "DO IT FOR THE MONEY"

In 1999, Alfie Kohn published an important book, ***Punished by Rewards***, in which he pointed out that all incentive schemes divert people's attention away from any inherent meaning, purpose, fulfillment or fun in the activity. By paying someone to

> Firms do not address the central question that non-participants have: "Why should I get involved in all this?"

do something, (or getting them to focus on the pay as the primary motivation for doing it) you are effectively saying: "Don't throw yourself into this because it has any meaning or purpose for you. Ignore those things. Do it for the money."

And, Kohn argues, people who are doing things primarily for rewards do them less well than those who are motivated by the meaning, purpose, fulfillment and fun they find in the effort.

Kohn reports an interesting non-business example. An experiment was conducted with two groups of children, each given some toys to play with. One group was left alone to play, while the other group was given rewards for playing with the toys (ice cream, cookies and so on).

After a short while, the rewards were removed from the second group. The outcome was (in hindsight) readily understandable. Those children who were playing with the toys for the fun of doing so happily carried on, but those who had been rewarded for playing with the toys had transferred their focus of attention from the play to the reward. If they were no longer to be rewarded, they would no longer play, and ceased to do so.

Doesn't this sound *exactly* like a group of professionals? Say "Do it and I'll pay you" and they will immediately translate it into "I'm not going to do anything you don't pay me for!"

What happens if people's primary (or even exclusive) reason for doing marketing is to get the money?

In *True Professionalism*, I first gave the results of a simple survey I have conducted (for more than fifteen years now) around the world. People tell me that they truly enjoy their work 20 to 30 percent of the time, and spend the rest of their time just tolerating it—viewing it at something they do (responsibly and conscientiously) to earn a living.

> **People who are doing things primarily for rewards do them less well than those who are motivated by the meaning, purpose, fulfillment and fun they find in the effort.**

Similarly, they report that they really like the clients they work for and find the clients' sector interesting about 30 to 40 percent of the time. Again, they serve the remainder of their clients with appropriate attention, but without any special interest, one client being much like another.

Notice that this is what people tell me. It is not my judgment about their lives, but their own assessment.

These proportions certainly help us understand why people aren't all that enthusiastic about going out, getting active and work passionately on business development. Getting more business just brings in more stuff they can tolerate for clients they don't particularly care for!

If you don't love what you do or those you do it for, why would you want to go out and get more of it?

The traditional answer is, of course, "Because they'll pay me if I do. They'll pay me to do stuff I have no feelings for, for people I don't care for!"

And that, of course, is the dictionary definition of prostitution. This is exactly the way many professionals feel when their firms try to get them to market themselves. No wonder marketing management efforts have such a low success rate!

If firms wish to promote enthusiastic participation in business development, they need to start talking and behaving very differently in their attempts to entice nonparticipants into the program. The very *purpose* of being good at business development, the very *reason* to do it, needs to be reexamined!

> **"They'll pay me to do stuff I have no feelings for, for people I don't care for!" And that, of course, is the dictionary definition of prostitution.**

What individual providers need to understand is that effort and skill in business development can help the individual find the clients they could care about and be eager to help, and the types of work that would be truly stimulating.

It's a circular, self-feeding process. The more you can really care about the work you do and the clients you serve, the more noticeable this will be to clients, and the more likely it is that you will be hired—by people you can care about for work that engages you!

The better you are at marketing, the more truly professional you can be, because you are not forced to take money from anyone and everyone just because you need the cash.

Go for things that turn you on and you'll get the money. Go for the money and you'll get less.

The trouble, of course, is that finding exciting work and enjoyable clients is not the reason that firms give their people to participate in business development. Skill in helping people find more fun, fulfillment and meaning in their work lives is not really why firms appoint managers, is it? But if firms want increased revenues, it should be!

CLIENTS AND "DO IT FOR THE MONEY" ATTITUDES

When *you* are the target of some other provider, how easily and quickly can *you* tell if they are interested in you or just trying to get your business and your cash? How easily or quickly can *you* tell if they have a passion for what they do—or whether they view themselves simply as solid, competent people just doing a job?

If you are able to detect these things when *you* are the buyer, how do *you* feel about them? Do such factors affect *your* decision about whether to hire specific professionals? How transparent are their underlying motives when they are engaged in selling to *you*?

My guess is that *you* can almost always spot these things and that, most of the time, they significantly

> The more you can really care about the work you do and the clients you serve, the more likely it is that you will be hired—by people you can care about for work that engages you!

influence *your* desire to work with such providers. It matters to 95 percent of the people I have asked around the world for more than two decades, and it probably matters to *your* clients too.

As it turns out, you and your profession are not unique even though you may think you are (sorry!) Your buyers, when they buy, are not that different from you and me when we buy.

"I'm doing it for the money" is an attitude most of us can spot a mile away—when we're the buyer. And nothing is going to make us less likely to want to hire such a person. Yet that is the number one reason firms give when they try to get their people to go out and generate business.

The message from management seems to be: "Do it for the money, but try to convince the prospective client that you're not doing it for the money."

Even if one leaves aside moral and aesthetic considerations, this is a bad approach. The vast majority of people are just not that good at acting. If the real motivation behind their marketing is the money they are after, it will inevitably show. And they will succeed less often, no matter how many training courses you provide to them about how to fake sincerity. Motives matter!

This is not an idealistic "anti-money" argument. When I'm your buyer, I don't expect you to apologize or be embarrassed about wanting the money. We all want the money. But if you truly want my business, then you will need to be a little more sophisticated about how to actually get it. You must win my business by showing me that you are interested in *more* than just the money. You need to prove that you are prepared to *earn* and *deserve* my trust and my business by being interested in me.

> The message from management seems to be: "Do it for the money, but try to convince the prospective client that you're not doing it for the money."

This is not news to us as buyers. Why do we keep forgetting it when the time comes for us to get hired? And why do so many firm marketing efforts seem to show so little understanding of how people actually buy?

HOW MANAGERS CAN **MAKE A DIFFERENCE**

A large part of the problem in many firms is that the culture and reward systems are built on transaction approaches, not relationship-building concepts. All that many firms measure is whether or not the deal was done or the project won—the outcome. They do not focus on helping people with the (logically prior) stages of building toward success.

For example, there is no credit within the systems or culture of many firms for marketing contributions that cannot be linked to "winning" a specific piece of business.

There is no "origination credit" for writing a good article or putting on a good seminar. There is no bonus for contributing a new tax idea that everyone else in the firm got to share with their clients. Unless *you* were the one to tell *your* client and *you* were the one who got the "here's a deal" call from the client, you don't get acknowledged.

Not surprisingly, this mentality leads everyone to under invest in articles, seminars, innovative ideas and the like, and rush instead to "selling" activities. People focus on the final event of trying to get hired, rather than the "romance" of successfully laying the groundwork by tempting the prospective client into wanting a relationship. They start approaching prospective clients with an overeager rush of "Do you want to do it?"—which is not usually a recipe for success!

Firms also mismanage marketing by fervently preaching team efforts (such as cross-discipline approaches to key clients) while clearly running reward systems based on individual performance. If you pay me for what I

Make up your mind, management! What do you really want me to do?

do personally, I'm not going to be silly enough to waste my time on any team efforts that don't have my name attached. Make up your mind, management! What do you *really* want me to do?

Firms also try to encourage their people to make personal investments in long-term relationships while visibly running short-term focused management and reward systems. Again the paradox or contradiction is soon spotted. You say you want us to do all the right things to build long term relationships, but you also want to reserve the right to be short-term decision makers yourselves? Come on! Get real, guys!

What all these problems have in common is that firms are not only "in it only for the money," but they want the money *now*! As a result, while they talk a good game about long-term relationship building marketing efforts, the truth is that these efforts are never really executed well unless they deliver results *immediately*.

Most firms' marketing problems are not marketing problems at all, but "management of marketing" problems. People are being encouraged to take approaches that everyone admits would not work on us as buyers.

If firms wish to be more successful at generating revenues, management needs to stop saying, "Do it for the money" or even "Do it for the firm." Saying these things cause many professionals (particularly the novices who need the most help) to profoundly misunderstand what actually works in business development. As Alfie Kohn points out, saying these things draw people's attention away from the true reasons they should want to be enthusiastically involved.

> **What all these problems have in common is that firms are not only "in it only for the money," but they want the money now!**

Management needs to start saying, "Let's do it as if we were planning to be in business for a long time. Let's do it to really be helpful and valuable to people we can care about, and let's have more fun and fulfillment!" Then they will be able to say, "Oh, and by the way, a wonderful consequence will follow—clients will love it and we will get richer!"

Pulling *that* off requires a whole new attitude about why we are doing marketing and selling, and why we work in the profession we chose. It is the job of management to create those attitudes in the firm (and to not generate precisely the opposite attitude, which is all too often the case).

Firms do *not* need to teach their people how to sell. They need to find out, person by person, what kind of work turns each partner on and what kind of clients each person could actually get interested in.

People can't love everyone (or everything), but if they can't learn to really care about *some kinds of clients* and *some kinds of work* (or the problems of those certain kinds of clients), they are not going to get a higher percentage of clients to give them business.

And if your people truly are interested in no one and nothing, there are almost certainly bigger issues at stake!

PART THREE: **MANAGEMENT**

The fat smoker problem is that—left to our own devices—few of us find the determination and discipline to do the things that will get us to the goals we have set for ourselves.

In the discussion of strategy in part one of this book, we have already identified the crucial contribution that skilled managers have to play in determining whether individuals or organizations actually get done what they say they wish to.

However, much more needs to be said, particularly about *how* good managers help to solve the fat smoker problem, and what characteristics they must have to do so.

Just as part one tried to offer a different view of what "doing strategy" is really all about, this section of the book invites a re-examination of what kind of managers are needed to bring about effective implementation of strategies.

As we shall see, good management is profoundly strategic if it can help individuals, teams and organizations accomplish more than they otherwise would get done. However, the key ingredient in this managerial added value is not grand strategies, structures, systems or processes. Management's essential role is to elicit the energy, discipline and focus that it takes to overcome short-term temptations and win by getting more done (and done better) than others do. They must also be the guardians of the organization's standards.

The chapters in this section provide examples both of the misguided approaches to management ("Tyrants, Energizers, and Cynics" and "Why (Most) Training is Useless") and of good practice ("A Great Coach in Action", "A Natural Manager", and "Accountability: Effective Managers Go First").

We begin with some common but ineffective approaches to making things happen.

CHAPTER NINE

Tyrants, Energizers, and Cynics

In my consulting and speaking (and through my website and blog) people repeatedly contact me saying things such as, "I like what you wrote in **True Professionalism** and **Practice What You Preach**, but do any real-world firms actually operate that way? Many of us are seeking what seems to be an impossible ideal: A firm that actually has principles and standards and doesn't compromise them for short-term expediency. Why are such firms scarce?"

For all of our grandiose talk of strategy and vision and plans, what we most often see (and do) is a philosophy that says, "Let me worry about this day, this week, this month, *maybe* this year. I'm under too much pressure to worry about next year." This chapter explores some of the reasons that we are all becoming more and more oriented to the short-term.

I f what I hear is accurate, many—if not most—professional firms have become less pleasant places to work in than they used to be. It is not uncommon for me to be told even by the most senior people that their firm's impressive financial results has been accomplished by a management team which is consciously creating an environment of fear and insecurity.

The simplest explanation for the prevalence of this "abusive" management behavior is the simple fact that, in the right situation, it *works*! It gets results without the delays and frustrations of having to worry about people's

> I like what you wrote in *True Professionalism* and *Practice What You Preach*, but do any real-world firms actually operate that way?

emotional state, not to mention the difficulty of developing the requisite skills to "manage people."

You can get higher performance out of individuals and organizations by being demanding, terrifying in manner, and (apparently) completely lacking in human sensitivity. There is, in fact, a time and place for this approach.

Think of a military unit under fire. Social graces are not exactly a critical element in motivating the forces to action and achieving team cohesion. Quite the opposite! In fact, bad language is sometimes used in such circumstances.

Using this approach does *not* mean you are being insensitive to people's emotions. Sergeant majors know exactly what they are doing when they yell at raw recruits. Rather than ignoring human emotions, they are demonstrating a highly developed sense of what human beings will respond to. It's just that they are deciding *which* emotions to work on!

For example, consider how you would interact with a child under your supervision who was about to put himself or herself in harm's way.

Would you be a calm nurturer, entering into a Socratic dialogue (in baby talk, of course) that leads the child to a deep understanding that certain things in life should be avoided?

No, you'd almost certainly scream at the top of your lungs, "Don't *touch* that!" and grab the child (roughly, if necessary) to pull him or her to safety.

> You can get higher performance out of individuals and organizations by being demanding, terrifying in manner, and (apparently) completely lacking in human sensitivity.

The child will cry bitter tears (as complaining employees also tend to do) but you will take great pride in the fact that you did the *right* thing. Appropriately, you will reassure yourself that more was accomplished by focusing on the outcome and not caring *at all* about the manner in which it was accomplished.

It's not a matter of being unfeeling, but of matching the appropriate temperament and style to the task.

Do you need results *now*? Do you have to show immediate results to please Wall Street? Are your heavy-hitting rainmaker partners threatening to leave you if you don't get firm profits up by raising the demands on everyone else?

Well, these situations are exactly like the baby putting its hand in the fire. This is no time for niceties.

At least that's how the "yellers" justify their behavior. In reality, it may just be that they are "do it my way or take the highway" people. But they can make a good case that their way is mandated by the situation.

Proponents of these tactics argue that they will get the best and, more important, the *quickest* results by inaugurating a reign of terror, instituting iron discipline, and putting in positions of influence people who know how to intimidate, scare, and cow otherwise intelligent people.

And, indeed, this is the best, most effective way to make it happen—once.

THE "EXCITING" **ALTERNATIVE**

The problem with this approach is that if it is used too frequently or even continuously, it begins to feel as if you are living in a world of nonstop, extended battles and wars—otherwise known as business as usual. Over time, it stops working.

As every parent knows, yelling and screaming, repeated too often, lose a little of their effectiveness every time they're used and they elicit increasing resentment. Nonstop battle, reflected in

> **Yelling and screaming, repeated too often, lose a little of their effectiveness every time they're used and they elicit increasing resentment.**

statements such as "We just had our greatest year ever, so we are raising next year's targets by 15 percent!" leads to fatigue and shellshock.

With lessened effectiveness comes the irresistible temptation to escalate the yelling and screaming in order to achieve the same results. Resentment builds even further.

People become worn out, suffer burnout, and leave. The troops, rather than rising to the rallying cry one more time, slump back into compliance (to avoid abuse), not the pursuit of excellence. The culture of the organization becomes miserable, if not poisonous. But take heart. None of this matters if you don't care about tomorrow.

There is another way. I began my book *Practice What You Preach* with the simple proposition: If you (first) energize and excite your people about the work they do (and the clients they do it for), they will serve your clients better; in turn, the clients will then (and perhaps only then) give you superior financial rewards.

I was delighted when my statistical data reaffirmed that firms following this sequence made (on average) the most money and grew the fastest. I could truly show that the key to superior profits was to "turn the staff on."

Note that the test is not, "Are your people happy?" That's nice, but not necessarily a profit determinant. What my data show is that the vital ingredient is the energy that comes from a sense of meaning or purpose and a common cause, direction, or mission.

If you (first) energize and excite your people about the work they do (and the clients they do it for), they will serve your clients better; in turn the clients will then (and perhaps only then) give you superior financial rewards.

The test is not whether your company *has* an official mission. The test is whether or not the individuals within your organization *act zealously* about that mission.

The conclusions always sound fine and dandy. Many people would be willing to accept that "turning people on" is a great approach that would eventually lead to greater accomplishments than the "get it done at all costs" approach.

But you'd only take this approach if you (a) truly wanted to get somewhere in the future, (b) were willing to incur costs today to get there tomorrow, (c) had patience and controlled your need for instant gratification, and (d) were more interested in building something new (a career, a firm, a skill, an achievement) than exploiting what was immediately available.

Those are a lot of conditions to meet! And most of them are about time and time orientation. To succeed by creating excitement in your people, you must have some rare qualities: the patience and faith to stay the course.

MEET **THE CYNICS**

I have run countless seminars exploring the conclusion that an excited, energized organization is demonstrably the key to superior financial returns. But these discussions have not always gone well. Apparently, there's something scary about the idea. Discomfort with, and resistance to, the conclusions take many shapes.

Among the questions I hear are the following:

"If we excel at turning our people on, don't we run the risk of creating unfulfillable expectations? They may expect to get promoted fast, and then, since we might not have the space for them, they will leave."

"Anyway, what's wrong with people not being turned on? Don't you need a certain number of people who are cruising (and *not* trying to go somewhere) in order to take care of the repetitive work that always needs to be done? Can't we just pay them less?"

Why can't we just set higher financial targets and enforce them, instead of worrying about things like inspiration and motivation?

"The people writing books say we will make more money if we require everyone to learn and grow. But *can* everyone learn and grow, or even become excited? Do we *want* them all to be ambitious, dynamic? Don't we make money off employees who will just do their job and not expect too much of the rest of us?"

"We can make a lot of money by just getting people to work harder. Why can't we just set higher financial targets and enforce them, instead of worrying about things like inspiration and motivation?"

"Time spent managing people could be spent getting out, winning clients, and billing hours. Isn't this a more certain path to success than spending valuable time trying to motivate people?"

"In books like **Good to Great**, business authors say that successful firms live up to their ideology and high standards, even if it costs them something in the short run. In today's world, is this really possible to do? Can we actually afford to incur short-term costs to enforce a principle of high standards? Can't good enough be good enough?"

"In the recent past, management penalized people who were underutilized. So, in down times, people hoarded work in order to look busy. How can management now credibly convince them that the path to success is to delegate familiar work in order to start 'growing their skills'? Won't people think this leaves them exposed? Would they ever trust the management of our firm to support them through a transition or an investment period?"

> The cynics create their own problems. Their limited, pragmatic focus elicits precisely the same reaction from those they manage.

People who ask these valid questions are not abusive, abrasive, or confrontational. But they *are* cynics and skeptics. They just think there's a (low) limit to what can practically be done in the "real" world. They say that the principles they advocate theoretically are unworkable in the daily workplace.

The cynics create their own problems. Their limited, pragmatic focus elicits precisely the same reaction from those they manage. If management doesn't really care about excitement, excellence, and the mission, then why should they?

Consider the message, the hidden assumptions, being communicated by the following (implicit) statements:

"We don't want you (employees) to expect us (management) to make any promises about your career progress. If you want to act as if you have a job, not a career, that's OK with us. We know we've hired some people who are incapable of learning and growing. We'll just respond with pay decisions. We want you to keep your heads down and hit higher work volumes. And, by the way, we're too busy with other activities to spend any time managing you."

Managers who have these "yes, but" attitudes send off very clear signals to those they manage. Even if they are never actually said out loud, these thought processes are immediately obvious in managers who think this way. And if your people think that you have attitudes reflected in the above statements, how do you think they are going to respond? Will you truly be able to achieve the excellence goals you say you want to aim for?

Cynics and skeptics in managerial positions are more dangerous even than the abusers. Through their cynicism they allow the abusers to be tolerated! ("Can we really afford to tackle the big hitter who refuses to show up for meetings?") Because they are tolerated, the abusers are never confronted and things never improve.

Although cynics and skeptics may not be as explicitly offensive as the tyrants, they are, alas, more common.

> **Cynics and skeptics in managerial positions are more dangerous even than the abusers. Through their cynicism they allow the abusers to be tolerated!**

CREATING **EXCITEMENT**

A firm where people treat each other with respect will in the long run make you more money, because respect can be shown to be one of the main profit drivers. But there's that escape clause—in the long run!

The majority of businesses in all professions and industries, have, unfortunately, become principle-free zones. Most firms would do anything for current cash, as long as it's legal.

Let's be honest. It's not just "those guys" at the top thinking and acting this way. It's everybody. All of us, you and I included. Of course, it's always easier to identify it in the other person.

For example, in almost every firm I work for, in every profession, in every country around the world, someone complains that the "new generation" is different from the way we were at that age. People tell me that the new generation wants instant gratification and they are not prepared to put in their time; they have no loyalty.

In other words, these senior people seem to be complaining, those awful kids are thinking short-term and not responding to our visions of the future rewards that would come from sacrificing their personal lives for (at least) the time it takes to become partner.

And clients can be even worse, I'm told. Instead of looking for trusting relationships, they keep asking, "What have you done for me lately?" Instead of looking to build relationships, clients are designing purchasing processes and competitive bid situations to extract the maximum juice from their providers at minimum cost.

> **A firm where people treat each other with respect will in the long run make you more money, because respect can be shown to be one of the main profit drivers.**

So don't just blame the leaders, managers, and bosses. We're *all* short-term thinkers now.

WHAT CAN **BE DONE?**

I don't (yet) know how to get short-term thinkers to become long-term thinkers. I've tried logic. It hasn't worked well on non-believers. I've tried presenting conclusive data. It hasn't worked well on non-believers. I've tried appealing to matters of principle, standards, values, and meaning. It hasn't worked well on non-believers.

I now wonder whether people *can be* "converted" on this topic. Preferred styles seemed to be well entrenched in people's personalities long before the age at which I meet them. The best any of us can do, probably, is to help the believers develop the courage to implement what they already believe.

To examine yourself and your firm, conduct a quick poll at your next group (or firm) meeting. Show people these three descriptive categories:

- This place is confrontational, abrasive, and fear-inducing.

- This is an energizing, motivating, inspiring place to work. We do what's best for the long term and act in accordance with our declared principles.

- We talk a good game of togetherness, idealism, and high standards, but the truth is that we're pragmatists. Cash wins!

Ask everyone to evaluate your environment by allocating 100 points to one category (if that's what they firmly believe you are all the time), or distributing the points across the three categories if they think you are a mixture.

The results may surprise you.

CHAPTER TEN

Why (Most) **Training Is Useless**

Many companies—if not most—use training as a business version of a "quick weight loss" program. They hope that by training people in new things, they can quickly bring about behavioral changes among their employees. It almost never works. As the article points out, training is a wonderful last step in a committed program for long-term change, but an almost useless first step, especially when it is being used as a substitute for changes in managerial behavior.

For much of my professional life, I have been paid to do training. It has been very well received in the sense that I have (usually) obtained high ratings, and clients not only paid their bills but invited me back to do it again and again.

However, I now believe that the majority of business training—by me and by everyone else—is a waste of money and time, because only a microscopic fraction of training is ever put into practice and the hoped-for benefits obtained.

Unfortunately, training and other kinds of meetings and conferences are too often organized as stand-alone events, with a life of their own, disconnected from the firm's progress.

What companies don't seem to understand is that, as I shall discuss later in this article, training is

> **I now believe that the majority of business training—by me and by everyone else— is a waste of money and time.**

a wonderful *last* step in bringing about changed organizational and personal behavior, but a pathetically useless *first* step.

Companies train people in new areas but then send them back to their operating groups, subject to the same measures and management approaches as before.

People can detect immediately a lack of alignment between what they are being trained in and how they are being managed. When they do detect it, little, if any, of what has been discussed or "trained" ever gets implemented.

A good example of ill-conceived (and premature) training approaches is seen in the many calls I get to conduct training programs to help people become better managers. I put my callers through a standard set of questions:

- Did you choose people for managerial roles because they were the type of people who could get their fulfillment and satisfaction out of helping other people shine rather than having the ego-need to shine themselves? (No!)

- Did you select them because they had a prior history of being able to give a critique to someone in such a way that the other person responds: "Wow, that was really helpful, I'm glad you helped me see all that." (No!)

- Do you reward these people for how well their group has done, or do you reward them for their own personal accomplishments in generating business and serving clients? (Both, but with an emphasis on their personal numbers!)

> **People can detect immediately a lack of alignment between what they are being trained in and how they are being managed. When they do detect it, little of what has been discussed or "trained" ever gets implemented.**

"So, let's summarize," I say. "You've chosen people who don't *want* to do the job, who haven't demonstrated any prior *aptitude* for the job, and you are *rewarding* them for things other than doing the job?"

Thanks, but I'll pass on the wonderful privilege of training them!

Here's a good test for the timing of training: If the training was entirely optional and elective, and only available in a remote village accessible only by a mule, but your people *still* came to the training because they were saying to themselves, "I have got to learn this—it's going to be critical for my future," then, and only then, you will know you have timed your training well. Anything less than that, and you are doing the training too soon.

THE **KEYNOTE SPEECH**

Most of the calls I receive about speaking at in-house company events are from companies that want a speech that is entertaining, informative, stimulating, or motivating. What they *don't* seem to want is anything that specifically addresses the way they run their firms or the real-world changes they are really trying to make.

For example, I recently received an inquiry asking me to convey to the audience the importance of living up to the organization's "sacred values" (including the need for collaboration). They wanted me to be inspiring.

However, when I asked if I could poll the audience as to how well the organization was currently performing on collaboration and what the current barriers to collaboration were, the organizers were terrified at the potential for disruption. I was not hired for that speech.

> When I asked if I could poll the audience as to how well the organization was currently performing on collaboration and what the current barriers to collaboration were, the organizers were terrified at the potential for disruption.

Very frequently, the person who calls me to discuss a speech or a training course is a conference planner or someone in administration—someone who is often the *least* empowered to engage in a discussion about *how* to bring about the changes that management desires.

The planner's role is frequently unenviable. Such people are often (perhaps even usually) given an impossible task: put on a development program that will change things around here, but leave management out of it!

The connection between management and potential speaker can be even more remote. For a few months I experimented with working through a speakers' bureau. I met with their agents to explain the type of work I was willing to take on. I was astonished to discover that my request was unusual for them. Most speakers and most clients operated on the principle that if the date was available then a booking was made.

Neither the client nor the speaker engaged in discussion exploring whether or not the speaker could advance the goals and changes that management wished to implement.

BUSINESS VERSUS MANAGEMENT

Another problem contributes to the minimal impact of much business training: the fact that it's about "business!"

> **The planner's role is frequently unenviable. Such people are often (perhaps even usually) given an impossible task: put on a development program that will change things around here, but leave management out of it!**

"Business," as a subject, is about things of the logical, rational, analytical mind: concepts such as "the value chain" or the numerous P's of marketing. Even when it's analyzing and discussing people, business is often treated as an intellectual process of analysis and discussion: Maslow's Hierarchy of Needs, the characteristics of great leaders, etc., etc. Business, at least as it is taught in our business schools and most training programs, is about *understanding* and *knowledge*.

Both of these are, of course, very important. However, managing is a *skill*, and (as it transpires) has nothing to do with rationality, logic, IQ, or intelligence. Whether you can manage is a simple question of whether or not you can influence individuals or organizations to accomplish something. It's about influencing people: singly, in groups, or in hordes.

No amount of understanding, knowledge or intelligence will help if you are unable to interact with people and get the response you desire. I know a lot *about* management from my education. That doesn't necessarily mean I'm any good at *doing* it.

The same tension between knowledge and skill, between rational and emotional development, exists in many other developmental areas.

Consider the topics of marketing, cross selling, building client relationships, earning trust, and providing client service. Many firms provide training programs and other forms of development on these topics as if the key problem is one of logic, analytics or understanding. However, as argued in part two of this book, the essential keys to success in winning business has little to do with rationality and everything to do with an ability to interact well with other people.

Becoming good at dealing with people (inside or outside the organization) is not accomplished by taking a college course in psychology, sociology, anthropology, or any other "-ology" where people sit around and intellectualize about "human resources" or "market segmentation" but never have to actually deal with a real, live human being.

The same, alas, is true of schools dedicated to the study of business.

> **I know a lot about management from my education. That doesn't necessarily mean I'm any good at doing it.**

Business school faculties around the world tend to be comprised of men and women whose backgrounds, inclinations and temperament are based in the logical and rational. They are well equipped to teach business, but are not structured well to develop skills.

If, however, we really want to help people develop skills, we must view "training" the way an exercise instructor would use that word—designing a planned set of activities that engage the right "muscles" and slowly build them up through the experience of doing.

To help people develop as managers doesn't mean discussing management (or, even worse, leadership) but does mean putting people through a set of processes in which they have to experience, try out, and develop their emotional self-control and interactive styles.

As Bill Peper, a facilitator within General Motors' Standards for Excellence process, reports on my blog, "Businesses often use training as a surrogate for the hard work of true skill development."

THE HARD BUSINESS OF **MAKING CHANGE**

Most firms go about training entirely the wrong way. They decide what they *wish* their people were good at, allocate a budget to a training director and ask that training director to come up with a good program. Training is too often used as a (personally) inexpensive way to look like you're doing something if you're a manager.

> To help people develop as managers doesn't mean discussing management but does mean putting people through a set of processes in which they have to experience, and develop their emotional self-control and interactive styles.

Bringing about change is immensely difficult and complex. Before designing any change program, it is necessary for managers to address questions in four key areas:

- Systems: Does the company *actually monitor, encourage, and reward* this (new) behavior?

- Attitude: Do people *want* to do this? Do they buy in to its importance?

- Knowledge: Do they know *how* to do it?

- Skills: Are they any good at *implementing and executing* what they know?

For example, managers could ask why people are not currently doing the things that management would prefer. Among the possibilities:

1. People view the activity as a long-term investment, and they're too busy looking after immediate pressures (SYSTEMS)

2. People feel more accountability and pressure for other things; they intend or would like to do the activity, but they feel they don't have the time to do it. (SYSTEMS)

3. People haven't been given the support, tools or training to do the activity (SYSTEMS)

4. People view the activity as discretionary, there are no consequences if they don't do it (SYSTEMS)

5. People think the firm wants them to worry only about short-term, and not engage in long-term activities (SYSTEMS)

6. The activity is not "valued" by their peers: the culture doesn't reinforce this (ATTITUDES)

7. People don't want to do it. They are more comfortable on technical topics, and not comfortable with interpersonal issues. (ATTITUDE)

> Training is too often used as a (personally) inexpensive way to look like you're doing something if you're a manager.

8. There is no perceived competitive pressure or threat in this area (ATTITUDE)

9. People view it as an optional choice (to be used if and when convenient). (ATTITUDE)

10. People don't understand why it's important (KNOWLEDGE)

11. People don't know how to do it (KNOWLEDGE)

12. People know what to do and want to do it, they're just not very good at it (SKILL)

As should be clear, training would be a "solution" for only some of these conditions. For others, it would be irrelevant. Note that skills development, as important as it is, is the last step, not the first. There is no point in offering skills training if there is no incentive for people to engage in the desired behavior.

The importance of the attitude questions is often underestimated. It is management's job to make people *want* to learn things by managing the "*why*"—helping them understand why this is important, why it is exciting and fulfilling, and why people should sacrifice their time and attention to get involved.

If you can be convincing on the *why*, the training itself can often be trivially easy. When people understand and "own" the importance of a topic, recognizing its purpose, meaning and value, and its role in their own careers, they often seek out (and find) the books, the videos, the on-line materials, and the college courses, without the company needing to provide them.

It is management's job to make people want to learn things by managing the "why".

In fact, when I conduct training sessions, that's what I focus on. I try, primarily, to get people *excited* about the topic, so they will leave the session actively seeking out the new learning for themselves. However, this only works if they believe that their company's management also believes this is important, not just that I do!

THE RIGHT **APPROACH**

The correct approach to training is to sit top management down and ask: "What are people not doing that we want them to be doing? And do we really know why they aren't doing them?"

Then it will be necessary to figure out a complete sequence of actions to address each of these questions:

- What behaviors by top management need to change to convince people that the new behaviors are really required, not just encouraged? If the behavior is going to be optional, then so should the training be.

- What measurements need to change?

- What has to happen before the training sessions occur in order to bring about the change?

- What has to be in place the very day they finish?

A full change program would include, at least, an examination of the following:

1. Scorecards (new, permanent measures of performance being trained)

2. Coaching (continuous monitoring and follow-up on the new metrics)

3. Tools (in place before the training, to help implement the training)

It is usually better to train people in their regular operating groups, so that the training can be action- and decision-oriented, with collective, commitments that can be monitored.

4. Training

5. Rewards and/or recognition for achievement

For maximum effectiveness, it is usually better to train people in their regular operating groups, so that the training can be action- and decision-oriented, with collective, commitments that can be monitored. Training classes that are drawn from different parts of the firm force the program to be "educational" only.

Large training sessions may be more *efficient*, in the sense that they expose a large number of people to the same set of thoughts simultaneously, but they are markedly less *effective* in bringing about change and hence, are much less economic.

Training should only be scheduled on topics that can be applied immediately. Too often, companies give people tools and techniques days, weeks, months, or even years before they'll need them. They hope the people will somehow recall them (and perform them!) flawlessly when needed. This is wishful thinking at best.

When outsiders are used to do training, junior people continue to speculate whether their leaders are really committed and serious about the topics being discussed. A firm's own practitioners usually are the most effective trainers. Although it is often viewed as an expensive use of high-priced practitioners' time, the greater credibility obtained when the firm's own respected people do the training results in much higher acceptance and subsequent application of the training. Outsiders should be used only to help develop programs and "train-the-trainers."

Even if the operating group leader is not conducting the training, it really helps if he or she attends the training as a participant. In fact, this should be mandatory. It brings an action-orientation to the discussion and builds in credible commitment to the program ("We're going to do this!") It doesn't matter if the group leader has been through the training many times before. Only the leader's presence can lend the sessions the seriousness they need and make the action commitments both practical and monitorable.

To ensure discipline, training programs should have mandatory pre-reading and pre-testing (whereby attendees can't participate if they don't pass). Yes, this sounds like a tough rule, especially when training senior people, but I have seen many firms that invested in highly customized programs, designed to bring about corporate consensus and change, where one-half of the participants prepared, and one-half did not. The ensuing discussion was an annoying waste of everyone's time.

The concept is simple: If it's worth doing training, it's worth doing it in a way that's going to make a difference. That means preparing and using session time wisely. If someone doesn't want to prepare, they should not be allowed in the room, no matter how senior. And if your training program doesn't warrant this degree of rigor, then you are almost certainly just dabbling and you're wasting a significant percentage of your time and money.

In 1994, I wrote an article entitled "Meeting Goals" (which can be found on my website) that tried to make clear that an effective meeting must not only have an *agenda*, but must have a limited set of clear *goals*. Many seminars, keynote speeches and training programs misunderstand this issue. Too many companies know the agenda topics they wish to cover, but have insufficiently thought through the goals they have, and how these goals are going to be met.

> **If it's worth doing training, it's worth doing it in a way that's going to make a difference. That means preparing and using session time wisely.**

The summary is this: If the training has been in regular operating groups, in carefully chosen topics, right when the group can use the training, and with the group's leader in the room, they can immediately begin a discussion of how they plan to integrate the training's ideas into their practices. With the right preparation and follow-up, training can be immensely powerful.

Without all this, it can be (and usually is) an immensely wasted opportunity.

CHAPTER ELEVEN

A Great **Coach in Action**

The two previous chapters explored some of the approaches that DON'T work in helping individuals and organizations stick to the diet and exercise programs that will get them to their goals. In this chapter, we describe an approach that DOES work: Ensuring that those in managerial roles have the attitudes, skills, and behaviors of a skilled coach.

I have told this story for many years, and referred to it briefly in my previous written work. This is the first time I have tried to capture in one place the many lessons from the story.

When I first joined the Harvard Business School as an assistant professor, I was not full of self-confidence. In fact, I was sure that I was a hiring mistake.

Rather than working at maximizing my performance, I focused on my immediate tasks (my teaching) and just tried to do my job, hoping no one would look too closely at my capabilities and performance.

For a while, this strategy worked. I was left alone. But after about six months, there was a knock at my office door. I opened it, and there stood one of my senior colleagues. "Hi, David," he said, "Have you got a minute for me?"

"Sure," I mumbled.

"It's such a pity that we don't have time to spend with each

> In this chapter, we describe an approach that does work: ensuring that those in managerial roles have the attitudes, skills and behaviors of a skilled coach.

other," he said. "You have your responsibilities and I have mine and they keep us busy. But I was just passing by and thought we could take a minute to catch up."

"Tell me," he said, "what's your *research* about?"

Since I wasn't doing any research (and we both knew that) I played for time.

"Well, I've been very busy and I'm not sure I'm really ready, and there are a number of things that interest me and…." On and on, I unfolded my excuses.

Eventually, as he remained silent, just listening, I said, "But, maybe… just maybe… and I don't want to make any promises… perhaps professional firms would be interesting to study."

He remained silent for a while and considered my answer. After what seemed an eternity, he spoke.

"You know, David, that's not a stupid choice! Now that you mention the topic, I can't think of anything major that has been done on that subject. There's a real opportunity to do something important.

"What's more, nothing in that idea conflicts with what we want to do as a school—I would tell you if it did. Well done! What a great idea!"

Then came the devastating follow-up question:

"And what subjects do you plan to research about these firms?"

I couldn't even pretend to have an answer. For perhaps the only time in my life, I was lost for words and remained silent.

I will never forget his next phrase until my dying day. He said, "I can see you haven't thought it through completely."

"But," he continued, "I know people at some of these firms, and I hear about a lot of the issues they have. Let me pass them on to you, right now, in case one or more of those issues interest you."

Most people I discuss this with agree that at this point in the conversation I had no choice but to select from among the topics he described.

He proceeded to describe a range of managerial and strategic issues faced by such firms.

Most people I discuss this with agree that at this point in the conversation I had no choice but to select from among the topics he described and say something like, "Well, I imagine it could be worthwhile to explore some of those topics with those firms."

He went back into silent thought mode. Finally, he spoke again.

"David, the more you talk about your plans, the more excited I get. This is great stuff! I can see it now. You'll do important work, get famous, and we will all be very proud of you."

"I'll tell you what I'll do, David. I'll have my secretary come by and give you a typed list of all the professional firm leaders I know. Feel free to contact them, and use my name. Tell them I suggested you call."

He then looked at his watch and said, "I'm really sorry, David, but my duties call me away. I hope I'll be able to come by soon and see how things are going. I don't know when that might be, but sometime soon, I hope."

And then he left.

Within ten minutes (*ten minutes!*) his secretary was at my door with a typed list of names, addresses, and telephone numbers of professional firm leaders.

Again, I had the overwhelming feeling that I now had no choice. There was nothing I could do but call those people. They turned out to be interesting and helpful, and I was on my way!

What turned out to be the thrill ride of a career had truly and finally been launched.

And here's the point as I experienced it: If he had not shown up, I *know* that it would have taken me a long time to get organized

With skilled coaching I was capable of getting more done than I ever dreamed of, and could achieve a great deal more when coached well than I could when left to my own devices.

and start investing in my career. I suffer from procrastination as much, if not more, than other people, and self-discipline has never been one of my strengths.

It turned out, however, that with skilled coaching I was capable of getting more done than I ever dreamed of, and could achieve a great deal more when coached well than I could when left to my own devices.

THE **LESSONS**

When I tell this story in my seminars, I turn to the participants and ask, "What was it about what he did and the way that he did it that made it so effective as a piece of coaching? How did he get this person (me) who was doing OK, but did not really have the car in gear, to get going and start being productive?"

(You may wish to pause reading here and write down what you think the key elements were.)

The answers people give are numerous, but almost always include the following:

The Existence of Real, Agreed-Upon Standards

Most people who hear this story observe correctly that there was no debate in our meeting about whether or not I *should be* doing some research. That had been determined long before, and was a precondition for his coaching to work. His sole task was to help me stay true to a prior agreement.

The role of agreed-upon prior standards in effective coaching is often poorly understood in professional firms. Standards in many firms are *aspirations,* not *minimum behaviors.*

Without unambiguous, nonnegotiable standards, coaching cannot work. Can you imagine the conversation?

> **Standards in many firms are aspirations, not minimum behaviors.**

Coach: "*I'm here to help you meet the standard.*" *Recipient*: "*I choose not to meet that standard at the moment."* **Coach:** *"Oh! OK! But let me try and persuade you anyway."*

The tragedy of many professional firms is that this is exactly what happens in coaching, particularly, for example, between and among "partners."

In chapter 5 I explored how a firm might achieve an unambiguous "prior agreement" on its standards. In this chapter, my discussion will continue as if your firm does indeed have such an agreement on standards.

Enforcing Standards

Accepting that there *were* real standards at the Harvard Business School, when did my colleague begin to enforce them? Most people would say, "the moment he knocked on my door."

It was not only the conversation itself that sent the unavoidable message that the standards were real and enforced. Perhaps even more powerful was the fact that, by his presence, he obviously (a) had been paying attention and (b) was able to respond in real time to my "departure from excellence."

The process of standards enforcement had already begun before he said a word. To this day, I remember both the feeling and the familiar phrase that went through my mind: "Oh, boy! Around here, you can run, but you can't hide!"

Of course, it is a common failing among professional firms that those in managerial positions do *not* notice issues early and do *not* have the time to respond to them in short order. Poor coaching is more often a matter of not having the time to do it (or perhaps placing other things ahead of it in priority).

It is important to stress that I was not (yet) "failing" or "struggling." My colleague didn't wait

> **Even more powerful was the fact that, by his presence, he obviously (a) had been paying attention and (b) was able to respond in real time to my "departure from excellence."**

to respond until I was "in trouble." He intervened while there was still time to help and influence me.

Essential to his impact on me was the fact that he had (or had created) the time and inclination to discuss my weaknesses with me, one topic at a time, right when they first became evident.

As simple as this preventative measure may seem, it is not that common or easy. Perhaps a majority of us in supervisory or managerial roles prefer to wait until the problem is so bad that we *have* to deal with it.

After all, we do have other things to do, and discussing with another person their weaknesses is not always our favorite activity.

I have direct personal experience with this. When I first set up my consulting business I faced, for the first time in my career, the task of managing someone—my administrative assistant. I had (at least) two big problems in being a good manager.

First, my assistant was basically terrific, so I felt that pointing out and discussing things that could have been done better was being demanding. (It is!)

Second, because I did not feel confident about my interpersonal skills, I was not sure I could provide a constructive critique and get the reaction I wanted. What if, instead of responding, she took offense and quit?

As a result of these concerns, like many other managers, I decided to say and do nothing. After all, she was good overall, wasn't she? Why rock the boat?

> **Essential to his impact on me was the fact that he had (or had created) the time and inclination to discuss my weaknesses with me, one topic at a time, right when they first became evident.**

I decided to save up all my critique and feedback for a full year, and then give it to her all at once, at "performance review" time, just like it said in the textbooks. (Or so I thought they said).

This meant that I tried to give her feedback in one session on seventeen different subjects, months after the events we were discussing had happened, right at the time when it would influence her pay.

Can you imagine a process less likely to get someone to listen, accept, and respond? Yet it's how businesses and professional firms do it all the time.

A performance discussion at compensation-setting time is the absolute worst time to get someone to engage with you, acknowledge a performance issue, and participate in designing a solution. By having the conversation at that time, you are asking them to put their income at risk. Even if they are aware of their weaknesses, they often cannot afford to acknowledge them at such a time, because they probably need the money.

Eventually, I learned the lesson we all have to learn. If I really wanted my assistant to improve, then the way to do it was the way it was done to me: dropping by on a casual basis to discuss a single topic at a time right when the weaknesses first became evident, and when it has absolutely nothing to do with pay!

I'm not saying I ever got truly good at it, but I did eventually understand what I should be trying to do!

Informal and Unscheduled

Anywhere in the world, whenever I have discussed the story of being coached by my Harvard Business School colleague, there is almost universal agreement that one key to his successful impact was that his approach was informal and unscheduled.

Most people agree that informal interactions have been most

> I tried to give her feedback in one session on seventeen different subjects, months after the events we were discussing had happened, right at the time when it would influence her pay. Can you imagine a process less likely to get someone to listen, accept, and respond?

influential in their own development. Very few people attribute much influence, if any, to the formal processes they experienced, such as annual performance reviews, counseling sessions, even training programs.

One of the eternal mysteries of management is that although we all know what worked on *us,* we keep putting in place other things (formal systems) for *them.*

The truth is that *all* formal, scheduled performance appraisal processes are doomed to failure. (See ***Abolishing Performance Appraisals: Why They Backfire and What to do Instead*** by Tom Coens and Mary Jenkins for a similar and more detailed view).

Performance appraisal systems in both large and small firms *may* serve to help arrive at a compensation decision, meet statutory and regulatory requirements for human resource management, or fulfill a host of other purposes. What they *never* do is cause performance to rise.

We have all lived through this. Only personal attention and coaching really help us (or them) develop.

He Talked about Me—and Only Me

Most people hearing my story remark that my senior colleague barely referred to the school (or the firm, company or institution) to which we both belonged.

He did not make appeals to my sense of responsibility or duty, such as, "Remember, these are our performance expectations here at Harvard, David. Let me remind you of your obligations."

For that matter, he didn't even talk about himself, his expectations, his reactions to my performance ("I'm a little disappointed in you, David") or anything at all except—me!

> **The truth is that all formal, scheduled performance appraisal processes are doomed to failure.**

The entire conversation was focused on me, which, of course, made it completely fascinating. He focused exclusively on helping me find what was interesting to me, not what was interesting to him, or what was needed by the institution.

Many managers think they have influence when they talk about what "we" are trying to accomplish, where "our" firm is going, and what the world expects of us.

All of this can be valid, but it ignores a profound human truth: The most fascinating topic for most human beings is themselves. (Apparently, I am not the only egocentric person in the world). Talk to me about me, and you have my full attention. Talk to me about anything else, and the odds that I will engage go down dramatically.

His approach was guided by a simple insight. If people set goals for themselves, guided by their own true interests, they are much more likely to pursue those goals with passion and to actually accomplish them than if you give them goals or attempt to tell them what to become interested in.

If I tell you what my goals are, I inevitably give you "nagging rights." You can ask me about my progress towards the goals I set for myself without offending me. You have the right to manage me more, and manage me more frequently.

However, if you try to get me to pursue *your* goals, not mine, then every time you ask about my progress towards *your* goals, I will feel resentment, and less will get done.

The point is meant to be a practical one, not a moral one. It just means that the coach will get better results for the institution if he or she finds out what the person is capable of being passionate about, and then finds a way to make that work for the institution. That way, everybody wins.

Of course, if the person is passionate about nothing or cares

> **The most fascinating topic for most human beings is themselves. Talk to me about me, and you have my full attention. Talk to me about anything else, and the odds that I will engage go down dramatically.**

for things that don't help the institution, then the coach's task is clear: urgently and actively help the person leave the organization and pursue his or her passion (or lack of it) elsewhere.

My coach asked questions encouraging me to choose my own goals, but it should be equally clear that I was not going to get out of that meeting without choosing *something*. There was indeed an iron will beneath that courteous exterior.

He Seemed Interested

Not only was the conversation about me, but my colleague achieved an amazing feat. He actually made me believe that he was interested in me personally! He seemed to care, at least a little, about me as a person.

I invite you to reflect, at this point, on your own reactions. Would it matter to you if someone trying to counsel and coach you convinced you that he or she was interested in and cared about you? Would it matter to you? Would it make a difference?

Ask the same question in reverse: if you doubted someone's interest in and care for you, would that impact that person's influence on you? I am bold enough to predict *your* answer: "Yes—a person's impact on me does depend on what I believe to be his or her level of interest in me."

If you doubted someone's interest in and care for you, would that impact that person's influence on you? How readily do you think you can tell if someone is trying to make you think that they care, when really they do not?

An interesting question arises. Can someone fake interest and still convince you that they care about you? Can other people make you think you are interested in them by learning the right skills, words and behaviors, or do they actually have to care?

Answer the question from your own experience: How readily do you think you can tell if someone is trying to make you think that they care, when really they do not? I can guess at your answer, but I know mine: You can perhaps fool me once, but not a second time!

In *The Trusted Advisor*, my coauthors and I explored this same topic in the context of dealing with clients, not peers or subordinates. It turns out that the issues and most of the answers are the same in all contexts.

As human beings, we accept the influence mostly, if not exclusively, of those we trust, and our trust is earned by true trustworthiness, not technique.

Unfortunately, most managers, when conducting managerial and coaching conversations, fail to convince the other person that they are truly interested in the person they are coaching. Very often because they are not.

He Didn't Criticize

At no time did my colleague say anything negative about me. He did *not* criticize me, even though a critique would have been fair and valid. ("You're not doing any research, and it is expected around here. Your teaching is improving, but you're not one of the best yet.")

Why did he not criticize me? Because he was such a nice person? Perhaps. But I think he refrained from it because he understood one of the primary truths about human beings, which is that *the absolute worst way to get someone to acknowledge and correct a weakness is to criticize him or her*!

As humans, we have a built-in reflex: Criticize me and I will defend myself whether what you say is valid or invalid, fair or unfair.

Later in our relationship, I did ask my colleague why he had never actually voiced any critiques and why he had led me to

> We accept the influence mostly, if not exclusively, of those we trust, and our trust is earned by true trustworthiness, not technique.

form my own conclusions about what he was implying but never actually stated.

"I learned long ago, David," he said, "that if two people both know something is true, there's not much point saying it out loud."

He continued, "There are better ways to get your point across. The key task is to create a way that the other person can concede the point without losing face. It's not easy to learn and to do, but it almost never includes explicitly criticizing people."

He Actually Helped Me

Many people comment that it must have been very motivating for my colleague to substantively help me, providing leads and contacts in order to get me started.

It was.

I have worked with people around the world for decades, and I frequently ask, "How many of you think that your manager, coach or supervisor actually *helps* you succeed (as opposed to demanding that you do)?" The proportions are depressingly small, as low as 10 percent.

Yet consider the psychology of it. If someone has just asked *you* what you want to achieve and has taken the first step to help you get there, wouldn't you feel an overwhelming obligation to take the next step? (For more on this psychological principle, see Robert Cialdini's book *Influence*).

The lesson for managers, coaches and supervisors (all synonymous terms as far as I am concerned) is obvious. If you want someone to respond to you, you must first find out what they want and help them toward that goal.

> **The absolute worst way to get someone to acknowledge and correct a weakness is to criticize him or her!**

Every time you plan to meet with someone to give advice, counsel or direction, ask yourself, "Do

I know how I am going to help this person in a way that *he* or *she* would consider substantive help?"

If the answer is "no," then you are not ready for the meeting.

He Focused on the First Doable Steps, Not the Ultimate Goal

Many people point out that my senior colleague did not focus much on the ultimate achievement or goal (e.g., "You need to write a book") but on small, carefully chosen, doable first steps: "Do you think you can call these seven people?"

As obvious as this is, most of us break this rule all the time. We try to get people energized and motivated by setting performance standards and turning the person loose: "Here's the world record—go!"

Instead, *tempting* someone onto the improvement path often requires that you remain completely silent about the full task ahead and just focus on immediate small improvement.

In fact, that's what good coaches do in all walks of life.

Coaches working with high-achieving athletes focus on one task at a time, reaching for small improvements in each area. They don't "raise the bar" in large increments; they increase it slowly and help the person make cumulative, repeated improvements. *That's* how you help someone become a world-beater!

He Gave Me Confidence

In another recent article of mine ("Management: What It Really Takes," *www.davidmaister.com*) I stress that you can't really help someone improve until you figure out why that person is underperforming.

In my case (surprising to those who know me now) my problem then was that I was not sure I *could do* research and writing. My colleague's (explicit and implicit) confidence that I could pull this off

> **If you want someone to respond to you, you must first find out what they want and help them toward that goal.**

removed what was for me (and, I am told in discussions world-wide, for many people) a major roadblock to accomplishment.

He Kept His Word

My colleague kept his word. He did what he said he was going to do. And he did it incredibly quickly. Because he kept his word promptly, I, too, was spurred into action. It would be impolite to fail to follow through with the list he provided.

Further, the cultural precedent had been set: you do what you say you are going to do. The message is clear: If you want your people to live up to their commitments and obligations, then you must first live up to yours. People will never live up to higher standards than their manager exhibits.

LAST **THOUGHTS**

This story confirms lessons that others have recognized and written about. Dale Carnegie's 1936 book *How to Win Friends and Influence People* remains the gold standard for learning how to interact with others. Blanchard and Johnson's *The One Minute Manager* is a fabulous place to start for those who are completely new to thinking about all this. And Peter Friedes' book *The 2R Manager* details exactly what a manager can say and do to be effective.

But there remains the Fat Smoker mystery: If so many people have offered such practical wisdom, and their work has been so well disseminated, publicized and understood, why do so many managers fail to actually apply all of this practical wisdom?

It's instructive to note that many of us frequently *do* apply the lessons and approaches described above, but we tend to use them more often in our personal lives than in our work lives. When dealing with family or those in our community, we are more likely to be informal, questioning, helpful,

> **People will never live up to higher standards than their manager exhibits.**

use the language of suggestion, and offer our confidence-building support.

However, we tend to restrict these habits to our personal lives without transferring them to the business world. When we care, we do things in a coaching fashion. When we don't, we don't. And in either case, we get back what we deserve.

CHAPTER TWELVE

A Natural Manager

Here's another example, in a completely different setting, of how a skilled manager goes about getting his organization to reach for—and accomplish—high standards. Ask yourself whether this manager of an exercise gym is using similar or different approaches than the example in the previous chapter in getting his people to stay true to the disciplines they need to follow in order to succeed.

As at the time of writing, Dyelry (Jerry) Labbate was the manager of an exercise gym in downtown Boston, managing four full-time and four part-time personal trainers. What follows is his description, given in March 2006, of his managerial approach, along with my comments on the lessons that managers can take from Jerry's experience:

"I never wanted to get involved in business. Born in Brazil, I have lived in the USA since I was twelve years old. I remember coming on the plane, not speaking a word of English, and asking the cabin attendant for some "agua" (water) and she brought me some Sprite. I thought to myself, "This is going to be a great country: You ask for water and you get Sprite. Wow!

"I got my undergraduate degree as an exercise physiologist, went

This is going to be a great country: You ask for water and you get Sprite. Wow!

to work at a major chain of gyms, and then moved on to the place I work now.

"When I took over, the staff was dissatisfied with their hours, how they were being treated and cared for, their scheduling, and their pay.

"A trainer would typically work from 6 a.m. until 8 p.m., with some hours off during the day. Even if you didn't have a client, the owners wanted you to stay on the premises until quitting time. They would do things like make an appointment without telling you, so that you had to change your personal plans.

"I've always believed that this is a business that is run by the trainers. If they do things right, your business will flourish. So to make money, I had to increase the level of service to the clients, and the only way to do that was to improve the quality of the job for the trainers. I had to change the environment they were working in.

"Before I came here, the owners did all the hiring of the trainers. I went to them and made my case that I couldn't really manage the business well unless I could choose people I believed in, people I thought could meet my standards, and people who would operate the way I wanted them to operate.

"I didn't want to insult the owners, but I put my case in terms of improving their bottom line. I told the owners, 'You're not in the center of all this. I am. I know everyone's personality. I can figure out who will communicate well with the other trainers and who won't.'

> To make money, I had to increase the level of service to the clients, and the only way to do that was to improve the quality of the job for the trainers.

"Anyway, the owners, to their credit, accepted my argument and let me do my own hiring.

"When I first came in, all three of the existing trainers were just in the process of giving their notices of resignation because of the way they had been treated. I persuaded two of them to postpone their departure so I could do some new hiring.

"Actually, the first new hire after I came in was someone whom the owners had selected, but I could see that he had what it took to do well. I liked him right away. The owners then told me they had hired a second guy. When I asked him about what he wanted to do with his career, it was clear that our gym was obviously just a transitional job for him.

"I told the owners it wasn't going to work. The owners said, 'Give it six to twelve months.' I did work with the guy, and he did become a good trainer. I supported him in getting his certification, knowing that it would only speed up the day he would resign to move on, and that's exactly what happened.

"I had two part-timers I could use, but I knew I needed to begin hiring.

"In this industry there is a lot of 'bait and switch' with employees. They are told one thing before they are hired, but then discover that the reality is different once they begin work. For example, people are promised forty-hour workweeks, but the reality is that it is almost always closer to sixty-hour weeks. It's common for every single person on the staff to feel cheated within weeks of coming to work.

"Trainers are a special kind of person. They have strong personalities, they are athletic, they play sports, and as a result some of them can be a little rough around the edges in dealing with clients.

"I only wanted to hire people who shared my philosophy of personal training. Some gyms and some trainers are just out to get clients to sign up for more classes, but I'm committed to passing on the knowledge I have about exercise, fitness, the body, and health.

> **I only wanted to hire people who shared my philosophy of personal training.**

"I believe that you train because you want to educate clients for their lifetime. You want to give them things they can and will do on their own and use for the rest of their lives. A lot of competitors in this business just get caught up in the fitness numbers (percent of body fat, etc.), but it's not about numbers. It's about helping people integrate new things into their lives. I always ask myself, 'Can this client do this repetitively? Let's make him understand that it's a commitment he has to make.'

"When I hire people, I look for this attitude. I ask them, 'If you were not doing this, what else would you be doing?' I'm looking for people who feel passionate about all this. The body is so amazing, and the more you learn the more you want to know. The adaptations it goes through as you stress it and develop it are really fascinating, and when I hire I'm looking for people who share that fascination. When I ask an interviewee a question, I can always tell if I'm getting a rehearsed answer.

"I require that every new hire has a bachelor's degree in physiology, not just a certification. Many other gyms will only require trainers to have a certificate. Not here.

"I knew that I had to set out to make my gym the best, and that wasn't going to be defined as having the most operating sites—a common goal—but by achieving the highest levels of client satisfaction.

"My first full-time hire was someone who had heard from a friend that we were becoming a great place to work. It meant a forty-five-minute drive each way from his hometown, and I asked him if he could handle that. He said, 'No problem'; he really wanted to come to work here.

> When I hire people, I look for this attitude. I ask them, "If you were not doing this, what else would you be doing?" I'm looking for people who feel passionate about all this.

"I began by laying down my expectations with everyone. I was very clear on the hours expected. I showed everyone exactly how to clean the locker room, how to set appointments, how to talk to clients, and how to resolve conflicts. I created an evaluation form, which I went over in detail with everyone.

"It contains five categories: Punctuality, for example. My inflexible rule is that the trainer must be there before the client, so if it is a 3:00 p.m. appointment, I expect the trainer to be in the gym ready by 2:45 p.m. I asked everyone, 'Is all this clear? Do you understand my expectations?'

"I don't have a problem monitoring performance. If something is not being done to my standards, I come to them and I ask, 'Do I have to show you again how to do it? Do you have any questions on how to do it? If not, then I expect you to do it. It's black or white.'

"I devised a training program for the trainers. For two weeks, they have to be 'clients' of the gym and be trained by the existing trainers. I want them to have a healthy dose of what it feels like to be a client, and to think about how you like to be talked to, recognized, and responded to. Then the new people have to guide one of the experienced trainers through their fitness routine, so the experienced employees can help the new people and give them feedback on their training approach and style.

"While they train each other, a bonding takes place. They come to respect each other and support each other, which makes for a better workplace and a more smoothly functioning operation.

"I talk to my trainers a great deal about their self-growth. I ask them what their vision is for themselves and for their career. I ask them where they think our profession of personal training is going. Among other reasons, I do it to learn more myself. The people I hire are usually straight out of college, and they have heard the new things the schools are teaching and I want to know.

> While they train each other, a bonding takes place. They come to respect each other and support each other, which makes for a better workplace.

"To get a new person started, I ask one of our regular clients if he or she would be willing to be the guinea pig and have the new person as a trainer. I promise the client that if he or she doesn't like the new person, it will be a freebie —there will be no charge. I've never had to invoke that—the client always accepts the person and pays.

"The essence of training is getting people out of their comfort zone, and that's not only what I do with my clients physically—it's what I do with my trainers in their jobs. I have failed sometimes here, because not all the trainers want to grow. Some of them just want to train.

"Once a month, I get all the trainers together around a table. I give them the big picture of what's happening in the business, what's going well, and what we need to improve. I try to light a fire under them, telling them what the competition is doing, and I remind them that in this business you must re-earn your reputation every day.

"I ask them to contribute to the meetings. I ask them to bring a new theory of training, or a new idea for an exercise, or a way to deal with a specific client training challenge. We discuss client problems, physiology, and the administration of the business. For example, we had a big discussion last week about sit-ups, with everyone sharing their views about which muscles were really involved, the best way to develop the complete set of muscles, and so on.

"At the meetings, I hand out responsibilities for the things we need to get done: cleaning, renewals processing, etc. I ask for volunteers for each task (everybody has to do something above and beyond the training), but I'll assign it if no one volunteers. I rotate tasks so people don't get stuck with one thing.

> The essence of training is getting people out of their comfort zone, and that's not only what I do with my clients physically—it's what I do with my trainers in their jobs.

"I always ask them, 'Is there anything I can do as the manager to make your job better? If you don't tell me what's wrong, I can't help to fix it.' Last week, at a meeting that the owners attended, I told the group that I was going to leave the room so they could discuss my performance and then give me some feedback when I came back in. The owners were amazed I would do that, but it worked very well.

"The main thing the part-time people said was that they wanted more help getting more bookings with clients. So I walked them through the difficulties (their part-time schedule may not match the weekly schedule the client has, so matching them up is difficult) and I told them I would do my best for them, but I could not promise to make the problem go away completely.

"The part-time staff is one of my areas of weakness so far. I should spend more time and creativity with them, to make them feel more a part of the team we have created.

"In 2004, the owners realized they had to do something about compensation. A normal target for a trainer is to have thirty-two appointments per week, plus eight hours of 'coverage,' i.e., other duties in the gym. I presented an idea of a bonus structure if the trainer saw more than a certain number of clients per week. It was modified a little, but it was accepted and it has really pleased the staff.

"I don't have control of salaries here, so it's hard for me to discuss them with the trainers. I tell them, 'If you want more, then show me the extra performance that I can tell the owners about. Help me create the reasons and make the case, so I can go to the owners on your behalf and fight for you.'

"I had one trainer who just wasn't a team player—he didn't share his load in cleaning up after

> Is there anything I can do as the manager to make your job better? If you don't tell me what's wrong, I can't help to fix it.

himself and so on. He was very knowledgeable, but he wasn't doing what I believe in—sharing his knowledge with his clients.

"I told him these things had to be improved or we would have to part—I don't compromise my standards. He said, 'I can't do that.' So we sat down and explored his options. I said, 'I don't WANT you to leave, I like you. But if you can't meet my standards, you're not going to fit in around here.' I continued to work with him, because I wanted to make sure everyone got a fair chance.

"After four months, I stopped assigning him work. He didn't take it well. He said, 'It's not fair, I'm a great trainer.' I said, 'Yes, you are. But you're not a great employee.'

"I want all my trainers to become great employees so that if they leave here and go to work somewhere else, the next employer will say, 'He (or she) was well trained.' Eventually he got it, and he left with no bad feelings.

"I think with all of this we have created a welcoming atmosphere for our clients. We think we have created something they want to be part of. It's very professional and we don't fool around with our training, but it's not an intimidating place.

"It's not a complex process. I have a rule that every trainer must know every client's name within two or three days, whether he works with that person or not. (We have about one hundred clients.) I want everyone to watch what other clients are doing in their training. That way, if the client's regular trainer can't make it, any other trainer can pick it up and know the exercises and the levels that the client is used to.

"I also changed the health history and chart system, so that if we have to substitute a trainer, there will be no problems knowing the special needs of each client. I am constantly in touch with all of our clients, making sure that

> He said, 'It's not fair, I'm a great trainer.' I said, 'Yes, you are. But you're not a great employee.'

if they have even the smallest concern, it is easy and comfortable to talk directly to me about it.

"I am now being asked by the owners to train the trainers and managers in the other locations.

"I'm personally doing about thirty client appointments a week, and then, on average, working an additional thirty hours managing the business.

"We now have four full-time and four part-time trainers, 107 clients, and 159 appointments per week. That's 33 percent more business than the same time last year. And it is growing still. The owners are very happy with the turnaround."

THE **LESSONS**

Both as a business school professor and as a consultant, it has been my job to teach people how to be effective managers and how to build successful businesses. Jerry seems to have figured it out on his own.

Jerry implicitly refers to some commonly taught management principles (I won't inventory them all—can you add to the list?):

- The key to giving your clients a great experience is making your people want to give that to them.

- You can't delight the clients with unhappy people.

- Hiring people who share your philosophy, values, point of view, and approach makes managing them a lot easier. Be very clear about what your philosophy is.

- The key to successful management is in the hiring: If you don't get the right people "on and off the bus" right up front, you won't be able to implement your strategy.

> **Hiring people who share your philosophy, values, point of view, and approach makes managing them a lot easier.**

- Hire for passion and attitude.

- Never compromise hiring standards just to meet a volume need. Set high minimums in entry qualifications.

- To get the best out of people, have clear, enforced standards and an empathetic, supportive style. One without the other won't work.

- Even if people are going to leave, take the high road in dealing with them. All your other people are watching.

- Never misrepresent, exaggerate, distort, or lie just to get something done, or to get someone to join you. People will find out the truth sooner or later, probably sooner, and there will be no benefit if they think you have misled them.

- You must help your people learn that there is more to serving a client than being technically skilled at what you do.

- If you focus on being the best, the revenue growth and profits will come, and your people will enjoy them more.

- Don't be soft—have very high operating standards that are clearly communicated and strictly enforced.

- Then give people the freedom to meet the standards without being micromanaged.

- Work at helping people actually experience what it is like to be a client—they will do a better job as a result of it.

- Work at team bonding by finding ways for people to work together and by getting together to discuss common issues.

- Learn from your people—let them teach you what they know and what they are discovering as ways to improve your operation.

- Commit to helping your people grow professionally: don't let them cruise.

- If you want people to be accountable, go first. Let them evaluate your performance, and let the results be publicly known.

- No one expects you to solve everyone's problem as a manager: All people want to know is that you're prepared to work with them to help them overcome the barriers and obstacles.

- In all of the emphasis on working with your people, you must never lose contact with your clients. Make it easy for them to talk to you and to raise any concerns they may have.

- Even though you are a manager, keep practicing your profession to some degree. It will help you to understand and relate to both your people and your clients.

Now, how's that for a quick and really helpful MBA course?

And, of course, all of these general lessons apply to other workplaces, even among highly paid people with advanced degrees in glamorous professions (though they don't always like to admit it).

The lesson is even more powerful. Without managers like Jerry, standards will never be upheld and strategies will never be implemented. The key to strategy is finding (or developing) more people who can do what Jerry can do.

CHAPTER THIRTEEN

Accountability: Effective Managers **Go First**

The argument of this chapter is simple to state: If skilled managers are a major key to an organization's ability to overcome short-term temptations and stay true to the high standards necessary for success, then how does an organization ensure that its managers are performing their role to high standards?

Acting on a suggestion I had made at a seminar, Jay Bertram, president of the Toronto office of the global advertising agency TBWA returned to his office and immediately asked all his people to evaluate their overall job satisfaction, their feelings about the office and (most critically) their overall rating of him as a manager.

Then he dropped the biggest bombshell: As I had recommended, he announced to all his staff that if he did not improve in their ratings across all three measures—by 20 percent within one year—he would resign! He later wrote the following to me:

"I was thoroughly moved by your passionate plea for senior management accountability. I want

> As I had recommended, he announced to all his staff that if he did not improve in their ratings across all three measures—by 20 percent within one year—he would resign!

to thank you for encouraging me to be a better manager. It is because of you that I am making a real difference for my employees. I have never been happier and more productive. I have just completed the follow-up survey, and my scores have improved.

"The results have been terrific. The office continues to grow rapidly and our employee satisfaction results are all above the corporate averages. We have become a better management team at having direct conversations with our employees, and we face issues rather than avoid them. I believe that everyone in the office has become more accountable. They look at what they have done or contributed before complaining about others."

What had I said that made Jay act on all this? He told me:

"You challenged me to be personally accountable for my role as a manager. It struck home when you said that many managers are seen by their people as lying—to others and to themselves—when they publicly proclaim their commitment to standards of excellence or missions for their organization and do not follow through. You gave me the reassurance that living up to my standards, and being prepared to be personally accountable for them, was the right thing to do.

"Every manager has room for significant improvement. We must challenge ourselves to stretch past our comfort zone by stating a goal that will generate a real change in our own behavior for all to see and experience. Managing is truly a race with no finish line. We must keep moving, learning, listening, acting, and growing if we are to fulfill our role."

When trying to get an organization to move, there is nothing more powerful than a manager who is prepared to lead—by going first!

Jay described my recommendation as "the right thing to do," and maybe it was, but in my seminar I hadn't been trying to make a moral point (at least not at that time) but a practical, pragmatic one. When trying to get an organization to move, there is nothing more powerful than a manager who is prepared to lead—by going first!

We cannot expect an organization to raise its game, change its direction or pursue new, ambitious goals and strategies by saying "Charge! I want all of you, the troops, to climb out of your foxholes and go put yourselves in harm's way." Realistically, that's unlikely to work. Instead of saying "Charge!" we need to say "Follow me!" We must energize others through our own example.

Regardless of any organization's purpose, scale or location, there is great power in creating a culture of accountability. When people in an organization can depend upon the fact that everyone else will keep his or her word and perform the duties and tasks each has accepted, more will get done with less explicit oversight. People will feel a heightened sense of responsibility and will act on it.

And if we want others to perform *their* roles to higher levels, we must ensure that they know and believe that managers are truly being held responsible for performing *their* role effectively.

The general point is worth emphasizing: to increase the likelihood that we will do the things that we know are good for us, systems of accountability are very effective. Perhaps even essential.

A SPECIFIC **RECOMMENDATION**

There are four steps toward making yourself accountable, and in turn, improving your organization:

Step One: Examine the specific statements below, one by one, and ask yourself whether or not doing well on each of these is an important part of your role—is it something you are *supposed* to be good at?

Instead of saying "Charge!" we need to say "Follow me!"

YOU, MY MANAGER...

- Act and live by the principles you advocate

- Act as a role model that people want to copy

- Are a person of integrity

- Enforce the company values

- Are a "part of the team" as opposed to being the boss, separate and detached

- Cause me to stretch for performance goals

- Are concerned about long-term issues, not just short-term profits

- Provide constructive feedback that helps me improve my performance

- Are a source of creative ideas about our business

- Help me to grow and develop

- Make me feel that I am a member of a well-functioning team

- Emphasize cooperation as opposed to competitiveness between work groups

- Are prompt in dealing with underperformance and underperformers

- Keep me informed about the things I need to know to perform my role properly

- Encourage me to initiate tasks or projects I think are important

- Are good at keeping down the level of politics and politicking

- Are more often encouraging than critical

- Are fair in dealings with employees

- Are consultative in your decision making

- Act more like a coach than a boss

- Are publicly generous with credit

- Are effective in listening

Eliminate from this list any statements that you think are idealistic, unimportant or not part of your role. Add statements (or criteria) that I have missed that you think you need to be good at in order to performing your role effectively.

Take this first step seriously and slowly. The purpose is to think through what you *really* need to be good at if you are to be an effective manager. Identify and discuss the key personal performance standards that are truly required in your role.

Notice that you will be trying to uncover performance standards for managers that will predict the *future* performance of the organization(s) for which you are responsible. The purpose here is not to identify metrics that record managerial performance by looking retrospectively at the group's results in the latest reporting period.

Instead, the purpose here is to ask, "What would I, as a manager, have to do well to cause my group to perform better in the future? What do I have to do well at to *really* make a difference?"

Step Two: Circulate the final questionnaire you develop, asking everyone you deal with in your organization to evaluate you on the criteria you have developed. Have the surveys returned

> **What would I, as a manager, have to do well to cause my group to perform better in the future? What do I have to do well at to really make a difference?**

to a disinterested third party (inside or outside your organization) to give everyone the comfort and confidence that the individual responses will be treated confidentially.

Step Three: Publish the average ratings you receive to *everyone* in your organization. Everyone—administrative staff included!

Step Four: Call a meeting of those you manage and give the following speech:

"Here's what you think about me. Don't expect me to be perfect the first time we try this. Perfection is not a standard you can hold me to, and it's not a standard anyone can hold any one of you to.

"What's more, don't expect me to be perfect a year from now when we repeat this, just as I will not expect you to be perfect. I don't think that's a realistic standard for any of us.

"But here's my promise to you, right here, right now. If, in one year, I have not improved my performance on the agreed-upon standards that are embedded in my role, then I will step down from my role as the manager of the group.

"You do have a right to expect that I will get better at the things that are my responsibility. And that's exactly what I'm going to ask of you!"

Now *that's* going first! Can you imagine the impact?

> Here's my promise to you, right here, right now. If, in one year, I have not improved my performance on the agreed-upon standards that are embedded in my role, then I will step down from my role as the manager of the group.

THE BENEFITS OF THIS APPROACH

For a group that already supported the manager, this would serve as a call to arms. In a situation in which the group mistrusted its manager, or doubted the manager's follow-through, the manager's courage in making such a public commitment just might be the action that could turn things around.

Why do I advocate what seems to be such an extreme approach? Let's analyze some of the many things that this process accomplishes:

- It clarifies your role as a manager, in advance, in everyone's eyes.

- It establishes the principles of accountability and continuous improvement.

- It creates a balanced scorecard.

- It provides feedback for improvement.

- It reduces the emotional distance between manager and organization.

Clarifying Your Role as a Manager

It may be debated at great length whether the sample questions I gave above are the right ones for you. In fact, depending upon the size and type of organization you are responsible for, I may have missed the mark completely. That doesn't matter too much.

What does matter crucially to your effectiveness is that both your superiors and subordinates understand and agree with the role you are supposed to perform, and the criteria by which you will be evaluated. In many organizations, there is a great deal of ambiguity about how the manager is supposed to make a difference. Managers are pressured to focus on a wide array of concerns: finance and administration, representing their organization externally, personal production of various kinds, and energizing their group.

But if there is no shared understanding of how you, the manager, are supposed to have an impact, how can you be sure that you are approaching the job in the right way?

But if there is no shared understanding of how you, the manager, are supposed to have an impact, how can you be sure that you are approaching the job in the right way? The very act of clarifying your role and obtaining others' consensus and buy-in can be a giant first step in improving your performance and that of those you manage.

Continuous Improvement

The approach of accountability presented here is not meant to be brutal or threatening. Rather, it recognizes that accountability means the obligation to improve, not to be perfect. Don't scare me about how demanding you are as a manager. By showing that you expect improvement but in doable, reasonable amounts, I am much more likely to become an eager participant than if I feel you have impossible standards.

Creating a Balanced Scorecard

One of the reasons that the managerial role so often goes neglected (and remains misunderstood) is that most organizations already have very powerful scorecards for other roles managers are asked to play.

Without the "upward evaluation" system described here, it is normal that managers will emphasize other, more visible, scorecards that judge how well they are doing: financial measurements, measures of volume such as number of customers or subscribers, user satisfaction scores, and so on.

The very act of clarifying your role and obtaining others' consensus and buy-in can be a giant first step in improving your performance and that of those you manage.

Some organizations and managers may claim that because they have 360-degree feedback programs, they already have the system described here. Many of these programs collect feedback from those being managed and subtly pass it on to the manager on deep background, without public accountability. But without public disclosure of the results, those being managed will be unconvinced that the information is being acted upon (and frequently they're right). That is not the system I am advocating.

The goal of a feedback system is not to measure or (just) to obtain feedback. The goal is to create a form of accountability that will both create sufficient pressure to improve and demonstrate management's willingness to be personally accountable. *Visibility* is a key component of *accountability.*

Obtaining Feedback on our Performance as Managers

Obviously, a consequence of the system of accountability that I advocate is that managers open themselves up to receive direct feedback on how they are doing as managers, and get the opportunity to consider ways they can improve.

At all levels of our careers, continued effectiveness and improvement depends not only on what we think of ourselves, but on what other people—those we are trying to influence—actually do think of us.

Unfortunately, people very rarely tell you the truth about yourself, which makes it even more important that you develop ways to get timely feedback on how you *really* come across to the rest of the world. We must ask for feedback, and act on it, while there is still the opportunity to change.

When you're the boss, all of this is even more critical. As has commonly been observed, when you become the manager, people stop telling you things—especially about your own performance. If you really want to find out how you are coming across, then you need to find out not what peo-

> **At all levels of our careers, continued effectiveness and improvement depends not only on what we think of ourselves, but on what other people—those we are trying to influence—actually do think of us.**

ple have to say when they are in a logical, analytical mode, but what they *feel* about you. This is scary stuff, but absolutely essential to know if you are to have an impact!

There are, of course, additional ways to obtain feedback from those you manage. As Jerry Labatte (chapter 12) showed, it's both possible and desirable to ask your people directly for feedback on your leadership.

I'd add one more little "trick" that has helped me when getting face-to-face feedback. If I ask people what *they* think of me, they are usually polite (well, usually). But if I ask them if they'd be willing to tell me what *other* people say about me, I give them the opportunity to say things without putting them in the awkward position of criticizing me to my face. Quite often, they say "Well, now that you've asked, David, there are *some* people—not me, of course, David—who think you could improve in these areas." We can then discuss it without raising the emotional temperature on either side.

The key point to note here is that although informal, more personal methods of obtaining feedback will usually yield deeper and more thorough insights than the questionnaire we discussed earlier, they represent a *complement*, not a substitute. Occasional in-person conversations may yield better feedback, but they do not represent the visible, powerful, "impactful" system of accountability described here.

Reducing the Emotional Distance

Perhaps the most powerful benefit of the accountability approach described above is that it makes the manager *a part of* the group, subject to the same standards and processes as everyone else.

> **When you become the manager, people stop telling you things— especially about your own performance.**

One of the most effective ways we have to get people to respond to us is to make them believe that we are truly talking about *us*. If we can convince people that we are all in this together, mutually committed and mutually responsible, it is much more likely that we will have influence.

However, it is remarkable how difficult it is to sustain this feeling. Even the best managers can become increasingly isolated, at least in the eyes of the rest of their organization. Managers can become resented by those doing the work, perceived as costly administrative overhead or increasingly remote from where the action is.

It is hard to energize a group of people if they view managers, as "*them, the bosses*," distinct from "*we, the workforce.*" Few of us are likely to be energized by (or can energize) those we view as being on "the other side."

Overcoming this distance and remaining part of the group doesn't mean that, as managers, we must do exactly the same things that we want our people to do. Some symbolic gestures are powerful, such as the owner of the hotel who bends down to pick up a piece of trash on the hotel carpet, thereby illustrating that he owns the problem as much as anyone else. But this symbolism can be, and is, taken too far. A manager can get *too* involved in the daily activities of the group.

In some professional businesses, for example, group managers feel that to manage effectively they must do as much or even more of the group's work than anyone else. They try to lead by personally selling more work and serving more clients. While this approach can (and often does) inspire others through the force of personal example, it interferes with the time required to perform the managerial role properly.

It's as if a military leader were trying to win the battle by personally killing more of the enemy in hand-to-hand combat than

> If we can convince people that we are all in this together, mutually committed and mutually responsible, it is much more likely that we will have influence.

any other warrior. It's inspiring, it's impressive; it may even be noble. But it's doubtful whether it's the best way to help the organization win. If you were a soldier, wouldn't you want your general to excel at generalship, and not (just) be the best rifle shot?

An effective approach must simultaneously inspire, create the sense that the manager is deeply embedded within the group, and allow and encourage the manager to perform the tasks that actually do lead to group success. In each of our organizations, we need to think through more thoroughly exactly how a manager is supposed to add value, and then we need to ensure that the manager fulfills that responsibility.

THE ROLE OF **INTEGRITY**

In clarifying your role, I suggested above that you should design your own set of questions, preferably in consultation with those you report to and those you manage.

However, it must be noted that researchers have explore which managerial behaviors are most likely to lead to future organizational performance. I will not try to summarize all of that research here, but it may be helpful to examine the findings of my statistical study of 139 businesses (reported in my book *Practice What You Preach*).

In that study, I identified the organizations that produced the highest financial performance, and then investigated how the attitudes of people within those offices differed from the other businesses in my database.

> **In each of our organizations, we need to think through more thoroughly exactly how a manager is supposed to add value.**

Consistently, the difference between the most successful operations and everyone else was attributed (by the people in the organizations) to the qualities of their direct manager. Such managers, they said, were the type of people who "washed their own cup." Their management was very personal, not separate, distinct or detached from their people.

The words used by these employees to describe the most effective managers in the most successful operations were:

- Honorable

- Genuine

- Noble

- Someone of high integrity

- Sincere

- Articulate about what he or she stands for

- Enthusiastic

In addition to these characteristics, the best managers were also demanding and set ambitious goals. However, being demanding and setting ambitious goals were quite common characteristics—such behavior was not distinctive among the most successful organizations.

It was honesty and integrity, as judged by the members of the organization, that *did* have predictive value (according to my statistical analysis) in identifying financially successful organizations. Managers of successful businesses, it turned out, did not necessarily advocate different things than other managers; they just lived and practiced what they preached.

At first, the "moralistic" words *honesty* and *integrity* surprised me. Why did these qualities lead to the superior financial performance I identified in my study?

> **It was honesty and integrity, as judged by the members of the organization, that did have predictive value (according to my statistical analysis) in identifying financially successful organizations.**

What seemed to be happening was that when the employees saw their manager demonstrating these qualities, they were more likely to believe and accept the manager's standards and values. The employees would then either join in enthusiastically—or leave because they did not want to participate in something that seemed so "inspirational" and "moralistic."

Those who remained had self-selected themselves as eager and willing participants in the ideology of the organization, and were more likely to function together as a team to pursue the organization's objectives.

There are many qualities that cause people to follow and participate with enthusiasm, but the honesty and integrity of the manager are clearly the pre-eminent number characteristics. Jim Kouzes and Barry Posner arrive at similar conclusions in their masterwork *The Leadership Challenge.*

This conclusion leads us to the ultimate paradox in all of this. I have tried here to make the case that the manager acting as the shining role model for accountability is a pragmatic point that leads, with high probability, to superior effort and excellence in others. Such managers can (and do) create superior financial returns—consistently. As such, this finding is practical, not a moral point.

But maybe the real lesson is that, ultimately, it *is* a moral point. Maybe what "accountability" *really* means is a willingness to be assessed and held to the standards one advocates—a point of principle, not a tactic.

> **Maybe what "accountability" really means is a willingness to be assessed and held to the standards one advocates—a point of principle, not a tactic.**

If people believe that the manager is behaving in certain ways *only* as symbolic gestures, then the act will lose its power. It gains in influence to the degree that others believe that the manager believes it. When excellence becomes a moral point, it will tend to be implemented better than when it's purely a pragmatic one.

In the final analysis, what would energize any organization is not the mechanics of any questionnaire, but the sincerity and integrity of the manager. Any manager can *say*, "These are the standards I believe in." What transforms an organization is when the group also hears the manager say "And I expect to be held accountable to the principles I advocate! Does anyone else want to join me in operating that way?" And they say "Yes, me too! That's what I want to be part of!"

CHAPTER FOURTEEN

Selecting a Leader:
Do We Know What We Want?

Previous chapters have tried to make the case that overcoming the Fat Smoker syndrome will require organizations to select, train and evaluate managers on some specific criteria; in particular, the ability to enthuse, excite and engage others to stay true to an agreed-upon ideology. This conclusion is not necessarily one that is currently understood in many organizations, but is important to discuss when the time comes to select new leaders. This chapter proposes an approach to conducting an exploration of what skills are truly desired and needed.

If you read multiple articles or books on the desired qualities of a CEO or a managing partner, you can get very confused. The list of desirable character traits, attitudes, skills and philosophies seems endless.

Job descriptions that many firms put together when searching for a new leader can also be confusing and contradictory. There is often a long list, including both "qualifying" characteristics that most realistic candidates are likely to possess, as well as a number of factors that will be possessed only by the best candidates.

Very frequently, the desired characteristics that are listed are in conflict with each other. For example, firms often say that they want their leaders to be both decisive and consultative.

> **Job descriptions that many firms put together when searching for a new leader can be confusing and contradictory.**

These are both virtues, but there is a risk that they can neutralize each other as a guide to choosing the best candidate.

Similarly, it is not uncommon to find firms who say they want leaders who are especially adept at being active *externally* (dealing with clients, shareholders, the media, and the community) and also be active *internally*: motivating people, readily available, and managing the firm's affairs. These two skill sets are not the same.

The situation can be made even more difficult. Many firms make lists of *generally* desirable characteristics of a leader, failing to recognize that the best set of attitudes, skills and behaviors depend on the individual firm, the specific opportunities and needs that the organization faces, and (for example) how ready the organization is to make changes.

After all, it's futile to select an Olympic-level coach for a team of people who don't want to play that game. There's no point appointing a skilled cost cutter if the primary strategic need is to grow revenues in new markets!

The bar is raised even higher for firms run on consultative "partnership" principles. Unlike companies that select their leaders according to the views of a relatively small board, the choice of a new leader in a professional firm usually requires taking into account the preferences, desires, and ambitions of a broad group of partners, shareholders or senior vice-presidents.

> **It's futile to select an Olympic-level coach for a team of people who don't want to play that game. There's no point appointing a skilled cost cutter if the primary strategic need is to grow revenues in new markets!**

As I pointed out in chapter 13, ("Accountability: Effective Managers Go First"), it is hard to hold a leader accountable if there is not a clear, unambiguous understanding of the role. Many leaders prefer it this way: they like the freedom of action that comes from an ambiguous role. However, as my co-author Patrick McKenna points out, leaders are, inevitably, going to be judged: wouldn't it be better for all concerned to know, in advance, and with clarity, what the true, real expectations are?

This seemingly obvious principle is widely neglected in practice. In many firms, in many industries, in many countries, I have learned, people are appointed to managerial positions without detailed consideration of the requirements of the role.

The need to clarify exactly what the leader is supposed to be good at is not driven (just) by ideals of democracy, participation or consultation. It's also about ensuring the organization's understanding and acceptance of the CEO's (or managing partner's) mandate. All too often, chief executives have been criticized, resented, and made relatively ineffective by being judged (both by their Board and those they manage) on aspects of the role they were not chosen to perform.

Many firms go directly to a discussion of the merits of individual candidates, based on a very general job description, without priorities established among the characteristics listed for the "CEO search."

If, however, you (first) have an in-depth discussion of what you seek in a leader, the weighting given to competing virtues can be discussed dispassionately, and not be excessively influenced only by the specific candidates involved.

A DIAGNOSTIC **TOOL**

Here's a simple diagnostic tool that can be used to facilitate your firm's discussions of the characteristics it seeks in a leader.

The questions that follow include a series of "paired" qualities that a good leader your firm might

> **All too often, chief executives have been criticized, resented and made relatively ineffective by being judged (both by their Board and those they manage) on aspects of the role they were not chosen to perform.**

possess. In each pair, either quality may be desirable. However, the point of pairing these qualities is to ask: if there *had to be a choice* between the two items in the pair, which would each respondent really prefer in a leader?

A simple way to "force" people to think through their preferences (and also to provide a simple way to aggregate the views) is to ask them to allocate 100 points between each of the paired items. Thus, if the respondent thinks the CEO should be mostly focused on the external community rather than inside the firm, he or she could allocate 90–10 or 80–20 to items in the pair.

So, what are the "either-or" choices you might present to your firm? As you scan the alternatives below, bear in mind that either side of the pair is (or can be) a virtue in a leader. The issue here is to set priorities, avoid ambiguities and conflicting messages, and force some clarity.

Do you want your chief executive to be someone who:

- Focuses on working inside firm *versus* focuses on a high profile with clients and marketplace

- Is good with numbers *versus* good with people

- Leads in accordance with a strong personal ideology of his or her own *versus* leads through tolerance of different views, values, and approaches

- Has a track record of generating business *versus* a track record of managing people well

- Thinks we need to make big strategic moves, even if they involve bigger risks *versus* thinks we should make small, incremental changes

- Has personal strategic acumen *versus* has the ability to facilitate and let others innovate and make strategic choices

- Has the best business qualifications *versus* has the best character qualifications

- Prefers to confront problems early, even if this can be disruptive *versus* prefers to avoid conflict until it's necessary to tackle it

- Focuses on preserving the firm's historical culture *versus* focuses on changing the culture to adapt to meet new challenges of the marketplace

- Moves fast *versus* acts deliberatively

- Emphasizes ambition and growth *versus* emphasizes caution and risk management

- Emphasizes reasoning and logic *versus* emphasizes emotion and excitement

- Acts and manages as a peer, a first among equals *versus* acts and manages as a clear leader

- Is primarily a "businessperson" *versus* is primarily "ideology-driven"

- Acts as the firm's "face" or "identity" in the media *versus* facilitates others achieving a high profile

- Is a fresh face *versus* is a known quantity

- Is very self-confident *versus* is humble

- Possesses a clear view of where we need to go and what we need to do *versus* possesses an open-ended view and will develop that with us after appointment

- Is a pragmatist *versus* is a visionary

- Primarily has a "hard head" *versus* primarily a "soft heart"

- Focuses on getting things done (i.e. a "driver") *versus* someone who focuses on getting it done right (i.e. an "analytical")

- Has an introverted style *versus* has an extroverted style

- Focuses on capitalizing on short-term opportunities *versus* focuses on long-term wealth creation

- Makes changes through dramatic, big moves *versus* makes changes through continuous, insistent pressure

- Sets the example of hard work *versus* sets the example of a balanced personal/work lifestyle

- Is diplomatic *versus* is "straight-talking"

- Is usually sympathetic to people's personal problems *versus* is unwilling to allow sustained underperformance

- Has a track record of personal professional success *versus* has a track record of building an organization

- Is usually trusting of others *versus* is usually not easily fooled

- Prefers to manage people directly *versus* prefers to work through others

- Is decisive *versus* is consultative

- Is hands-on, involved in the details *versus* is hands-off, sets the direction and then holds people accountable

Naturally, it is possible to adapt this questionnaire to your own firm, inserting pairs that I have omitted and deleting ones you think are less critical to your firm.

The key is to make the choices difficult, so that people are forced to reflect on what are the *key, top-priority* characteristics for the right chief executive for your firm, right now.

I sometimes use other ways to "force" people to indicate preferences. Instead of allocating 100 points, respondents could be asked to choose one point on a four-point scale for each pair of virtues:

1 = the leader should possess the first quality MUCH more than the second quality

2 = the leader should possess the first quality a LITTLE more than the second quality

3 = the leader should possess the second quality a LITTLE more than the first quality

4 = the leader should possess the second quality MUCH more than the first quality

Because we are asking what people to narrow their choice and reveal their true priorities, there would be no "middle or equal balance" option.

USING **THE TOOL**

Begin by circulating the questionnaire among the relevant participants (partners, shareholders or senior vice-presidents). When everyone has contributed their views, prepare charts showing both the weighted average view and (this is important) the distribution of views, so that it is clear where people are of similar minds, and where they have divided views.

An important educational, bonding and strategy-setting function will be served by using the results for a discussion of the differing views. The point of the survey tool is not to suppress debate, but to identify the subjects most worthy of debate. Areas

Areas of consensus can be quickly noted, and discussion focused on topics where there is a disparity of views.

of consensus can be quickly noted, and discussion focused on topics where there is a disparity of views.

For example, some participants may enter the process thinking that the chief executive should be a primary business-getter; others will think differently. Debate forges a better, healthier consensus about the priorities, not only for the chief executive, but for the firm.

One of the inherent flaws in any discussion of desirable leadership characteristics is people's tendency for "regression toward the mean"—people tend to express preferences in comparison to a previous or current leader, rather than against a set of absolute qualities. For example, if a previous leader has been noted for tilting the balance toward decisiveness rather than extensive consultation, there will be a tendency for people to vote for the new leader to be more consultative. And, of course, the reverse is true.

Once you have completed a first-round survey using these "paired characteristics," you will probably still have a lengthy, multi-item list of desired traits. You should then conduct a second round of the survey by creating new either-or choices from the surviving criteria.

Repeated rounds of "forced choices" may sound onerous, but eventually they will clearly reveal what kind of leader is desired. The benefits of recognizing and choosing a new leader according to clear, unambiguous, non-contradictory criteria will make all the effort worthwhile.

An important educational, bonding and strategy-setting function will be served by using the results for a discussion of the differing views. The point of the survey tool is not to suppress debate, but to identify the subjects most worthy of debate.

To facilitate the ability to take repeated votes, I often run meetings on this topic using audience response systems in which each person can quickly vote (anonymously) through a wireless, electronic keypad, the group results being shown instantaneously on a screen in front of everyone assembled.

The first benefit of such systems is that there is no requirement to pre-program the questions, and the time from phrasing the question to seeing the views of the group is only a few seconds. Because of this, if a vote is ambiguous, or seen to be poorly phrased, an immediate re-vote is possible.

Secondly, the ability to conduct sequential "rounds" of voting enables the group to test its key criteria. For example, a list of ten "surviving" criteria can quickly be reduced to the most important five or six by repeating the pairing process instantaneously, asking "If you could only have one of these, which would it be?"

Finally, the fact that audience response systems eliminate the need for a "paper trail." They store voting data electronically, so that the expressions of views that were made at the meeting can be referenced in future deliberations and decisions.

SUMMARY

This approach forces many people to reflect in depth for the first time what kind of leader they truly think is best for the firm and, perhaps more importantly, what kind of leader they are prepared to accept and be guided by. I have used it even with relatively small corporate boards of directors that needed to clarify competing criteria when appointing top corporate officers.

You may be surprised not only by the choices that some of your colleagues will make. You may also be surprised by the amount of unanimity that often exists, when "push comes to shove", in what people seek in a leader.

> **This approach forces many people to reflect in depth for the first time what kind of leader they truly think is best for the firm and, perhaps more importantly, what kind of leader they are prepared to accept and be guided by.**

After this exercise, your firm will be ready to examine your candidates, and choose the right leader for where your firm is today and where your organization wants to go.

PART FOUR:
PUTTING IT TOGETHER

The chapters in this closing section not only draw together some of the themes of the book, but also offer some further illustration and analysis.

If any firms have found ways to overcome the Fat Smoker syndrome, keeping their eyes firmly fixed on the long-term and acting together, it may be the widely admired "One-firm firms" that I first wrote about in 1985. In chapter 15, I explore (with a co-author, Jack Walker) what these firms have preserved and what have they changed in the intervening years.

Next, in an article coauthored with Patrick J. McKenna, I look at the complex structures of modern professional businesses.

I then look at the special challenges for formulating and adhering to strategy in a single profession: lawyers. At least, that's what I thought I was writing when I first published this chapter as an article. However, as I note in the introduction to that chapter, I subsequently heard (after its initial publication) that people in other businesses thought the topics addressed there were also relevant to them.

While some may disagree with my critical analysis about what may be taking place in a particular profession, most people will find common ground on the importance of the topics.

I conclude with two summary chapters—"The Chief Executive's Speech" and "Passion, People, and Principle"—each designed to capture (in separate ways) this book's themes.

CHAPTER FIFTEEN

The **One-Firm Firm** Revisited

In 1985, I wrote an article for the *Sloan Management Review* called "The One-Firm Firm," which identified a strategy common to leading firms across a broad array of professions—creating institutional loyalty and team focus. They seemed to apply many of the principles I advocated then—and now.

The firms named in that article were McKinsey, Goldman Sachs, Arthur Andersen, Hewitt Associates, and the law firm of Latham & Watkins. If you are prepared to accept the argument that Accenture (formerly Andersen Consulting) is the legacy firm of Arthur Andersen (and not the now-defunct audit-based business), then that 1985 list of one-firm firms stacks up remarkably well as a predictor of subsequent success. These are still preeminent and immensely successful firms.

In this article, coauthored with Jack Walker, formerly the managing partner of Latham & Watkins, I revisit the actions and performance of these widely admired firms.

The marketplace for professional services has changed in ways that were unimaginable in 1985. Clients and client relationships have become dynamic at best and fickle at worst. Shortages and mobility of talent have affected every profession. As a result, the five named firms—and their main competitors—have adapted by making dramatic and often risky changes.

For example, of those five firms, Goldman, Accenture, and Hewitt have become publicly held companies—most have acquired other firms with varying degrees of success, and all have grown, become

> Each has maintained or improved its competitive position as one of the most admired and profitable firms in its industry or profession.

global, and (except perhaps in the case of McKinsey) have profoundly diversified their service offerings. Yet each has maintained or improved its competitive position as one of the most admired and profitable firms in its industry or profession.

This chapter addresses the issue of whether the one-firm firm *principles* identified in 1985 are still relevant to the continued, sustained success of these five firms. It focuses on what has been maintained, adapted, and abandoned in their management since 1985.

As we shall see, one-firm firm principles do indeed continue to drive success for these firms, even as their specific practices have been adapted and modified for changing market conditions.

WHAT IS IT?

The one-firm firm approach is not simply a loose term to describe a "culture." It refers to a set of concrete management practices consciously chosen to maximize the trust and loyalty that members of the firm feel both to the institution and to each other.

In 1985, the elements of the one-firm firm approach were given as:

- Highly selective recruitment

- A "grow your own" people strategy as opposed to heavy use of laterals, growing only as fast as people could be developed and assimilated

> A set of concrete management practices consciously chosen to maximize the trust and loyalty that members of the firm feel both to the institution and to each other.

- Intensive use of training as a socialization process

- Rejection of a "star system" and related individualistic behavior

- Avoidance of mergers, in order to sustain the collaborative culture

- Selective choice of services and markets, so as to win through significant investments in focused areas rather than many small initiatives

- Active outplacement and alumni management, so that those who leave remain loyal to the firm

- Compensation based mostly on group performance, not individual performance

- High investments in research and development

- Extensive intra-firm communication, with broad use of consensus-building approaches

The one-firm firm approach is similar in many ways to the U.S. Marine Corps (in which Jack Walker served). Both are designed to achieve the highest levels of internal collaboration and encourage mutual commitment to pursuing ambitious goals.

Marines have a special bond and a shared pride, built on shared values and a shared striving for excellence with integrity. Every marine grasps the concept of stewardship—the organization, its reputation, and its very effectiveness have been inherited from previous generations and are held in trust for future generations.

Marines are noted for acting as a cohesive unit rather as than individual members. Each marine honors the corps' traditions: unity, pride, respect, loyalty, excellence, and integrity. The key relationship is that of the individual member to the organization, in the form of a set of reciprocal,

> **Marines have a special bond and a shared pride, built on shared values and a shared striving for excellence with integrity. Every marine grasps the concept of stewardship—the organization, its reputation, and its very effectiveness have been inherited from previous generations and are held in trust for future generations.**

value-based expectations. This in turn informs and supports relationships among members who may not even know each other personally.

Everyone knows the values he or she must live by and the code of behavior he or she must follow. Everyone is commonly and intensively trained in these values and protocols. Everyone also knows that if an individual is in trouble, the group will expend every effort to help him or her.

THE WARLORD MODEL

A contrasting, and more common, approach to running a professional service firm is the "star-based" or "warlord" concept, which succeeds by emphasizing internal competition, individual entrepreneurialism, distinct profit centers, decentralized decision making, and the strength that comes from stimulating many diverse initiatives driven by relatively autonomous operators.

In extreme warlord firms, the productive senior members operate as chieftains presiding over their own territories, occasionally collaborating but generally acting without a long-run commitment to the institution or each other.

Many prosperous firms who prefer the warlord model succeed by replacing institutional energy with the sum of individual entrepreneurial energies. They forgo institutional commitment and collaboration in favor of attracting and retaining the most successful warlords.

Warlord firms succeed when management keeps the "big hitters" happy and productive. The past and the future are not often items high on the agenda. Consequently, over time, the performance of extreme warlord firms often swings through peaks and valleys. Much management energy is expended in modulating the politically charged environment.

> **Warlord firms succeed when management keeps the "big hitters" happy and productive.**

Personal taste can play an important role in determining which path a firm takes. Some of the most effective professionals cannot abide by the one-firm firm model and thrive in the warlord model (and vice versa).

Most firms are neither pure one-firm firms nor pure warlord firms. What the two extreme forms have in common is a high level of energy. Firms in the middle may pay a price if they fail to fully engage either high levels of internal collaboration or high levels of entrepreneurial individualism.

Capturing the benefits of high institutional energy is not easy. The one-firm firm system (like that of the Marine Corps) depends upon a mutually reinforcing set of concrete policies and practices, and many firms may not be able to "get from here to there" in a short period of time. True one-firm firms are, and will likely remain, statistical anomalies in each of their industries, albeit successful ones.

TWENTY-TWO YEARS ON

If one were to focus primarily on their range of their services and locations, the five one-firm firms are now almost unrecognizable compared to what they were in 1985.

Goldman now emphasizes proprietary trading, a change from its predominantly advisory roots; Hewitt and Accenture have moved into business process outsourcing; and both McKinsey and Latham have expanded their service offerings and global coverage. As mentioned, Accenture, Hewitt, and Goldman have become public companies.

According to most press reports, McKinsey experimented with some significant changes as the consulting industry felt the impact of technology. An early countercultural attempt to

> If one were to focus primarily on their range of their services and locations, the five one-firm firms are now almost unrecognizable compared to what they were in 1985.

acquire and integrate an IT firm was generally considered to be a failure.

In the late 1990s, the technology bubble led the firm to expand at a faster pace, rapidly increasing the rate of hiring new juniors. The firm opened offices in many more locations around the world and reportedly cut back on training. As did other professional firms in that era, McKinsey stretched its compensation system to pay stars more in order to keep them.

Then, when the bubble burst, the relative economics dropped and (according to media reports) the firm had to downsize, issuing a capital call on its partners. However, according to most reports, the new managing partner who took over in 2003 has reoriented the firm to a more values-driven, one-firm firm approach.

Goldman Sachs has also been through significant policy and cultural changes, particularly during the late 1990s, leading up to the decision to go public. As with much of Wall Street, the traditional reliance on long-term relationships to build the firm has been significantly influenced by a move toward a "transactional" approach, pursuing fast-moving market opportunities. Nevertheless, most observers would concede that Goldman is still, by far, the most collaborative, team-based banking firm.

Latham has also stretched the boundaries of the one-firm firm approach. Like most of the one-firm firms, it has relied on an increased use of laterals. It has also introduced a greater individual component into its reward scheme. And it has acquired some sizable groups over the course of its expansion, adding, for example, a firm of more than ninety lawyers in France in 2001.

> **Despite these changes, most of the one-firm firms have retained their commitment to teamwork and collaboration rather than to individual entrepreneurialism.**

Hewitt has also experienced dramatic changes. A few years ago it acquired a large firm that was difficult to integrate. It has gone public and has shifted from being mainly an advisory firm to being primarily a human resources business processing outsourcer.

Hewitt often acquires the client's HR department in order to do this, which is contrary to the one-firm firm approach of stringent, selective recruiting from the bottom.

Accenture has also migrated to the profoundly different business of outsourcing, along with the concomitant less stringent hiring practices.

Despite these changes, most of the one-firm firms have retained their commitment to teamwork and collaboration rather than to individual entrepreneurialism. This is most clearly revealed in their special human resource practices, designed to enforce high standards of *both* teamwork and dynamism.

The April 29, 2006 issue of *The Economist* contains an article profiling Goldman Sachs, with rich details about its intensive and selective hiring and promotion processes and the enforcement of high standards even among the firm's most senior people. The article says, "Often enough, someone important is asked to leave. This is one of Paulson's most critical roles." (Then-CEO Hank Paulson later became US Treasury Secretary).

Paulson is quoted as saying: "Goldman is a hard place to be hired, a hard place to be promoted and a hard place to stay." One of *The Economist's* writers observes, "If you want an explanation of how Goldman endures, that, perhaps, is the best explanation of all."

What these firms teach us is that the essence of the one-firm firm strategy (and what gives it its economic power) is *not* a superior ability to select markets and services, but a greater ability to achieve high standards through the consistent application and enforcement of espoused operating rules, philosophies, values, and ideologies.

> A hard place to be hired, a hard place to be promoted and a hard place to stay.

THE ROLE OF **LEADERSHIP**

A key component in a successful one-firm firm is the governance structure. Members of the firm must feel that they have approved the leaders and that the leaders are accountable to them. This is normally accomplished by members electing the head of the firm, who then serve for a term, typically renewable by election.

In most cases, the leader is supported by a small, elected term-limited management committee comprised of practicing professionals. This accountability is usually balanced by a structure that insulates the leadership from the wrath of colleagues, following tough decisions that may involve short-term unpleasantness for long-term gain.

Because one-firm firms are driven by a commonly held ideology, once all viewpoints are aired and management makes its decision, the partners generally support that decision. Partners or senior officers are willing to delegate managerial powers upward because they trust that those appointed to leadership will operate in accordance with the principles and values of the firm's ideology. The existence of shared values underpins sustained management effectiveness.

Maintaining this environment requires active management effort and (usually) careful thought in the appointment of group leaders. Running on autopilot is not an option.

Peter Friedes, the former CEO of Hewitt Associates, said, "I had fifteen or so managers reporting to me. I needed them to not be pulling the firm in different directions. One practice I had was to remind all those who reported to me that part of their role was to have my CEO perspective in managing their group. They were not to just be an advocate for their group or their people. They had to have a 'whole entity' view."

> **Once all viewpoints are aired and management makes its decision, the partners generally support that decision.**

The payoff from this consensus, values-based management practice can be huge. It permits the firm to excel at getting things done as a firm. Partners in warlord firms typically continue to undermine decisions they dislike, since they feel that they have not delegated the power to management to make those decisions.

This doesn't mean that one-firm firm partners are shy about expressing themselves or opposing management as issues arise. They do, but more safely and effectively than in warlord firms, where political risk and retribution are real issues.

SIZE AND GROWTH

It is very difficult to sustain the one-firm firm, consensus-based governance system as the firm grows beyond the point where all members know each other. The good news is that many (if not most) powerful professionals yearn to be part of a cohesive team, often in spite of their chest-thumping behavior. This yearning is something that can be leveraged.

As clients and competitors change and as firms grow and expand, management must work harder to hold the firm together by, among other things, engendering a sense of reciprocal obligation both between the firm and individual members and among the members.

While twenty years ago a firm could engage in broad consultation and give people a real sense of participation, today's mega-large one-firm firms cannot feasibly do this without great effort and creativity.

Inevitably, the top person becomes more CEO-like. This has happened at each of the named firms. This predictable transition from consensus-building to a "consult then decide" approach can be

> Partners in warlord firms typically continue to undermine decisions they dislike, since they feel that they have not delegated the power to management to make those decisions.

successfully accomplished only when built upon a strong and long-established philosophical base of shared values.

In a sense, the trust given to the firm-wide (often global) CEO is a residual habit left over from times when the CEO was universally known and approachable. If the chief executive is to enjoy the same latitude to manage as in the past, then his or her character, values, and principles all become even more important. And, of course, he or she must continue to deliver. Shared values go only so far.

THE ROLE OF **SELECTIVE RECRUITING**

A core characteristic of the one-firm firm is the careful hiring, training, and indoctrination of new talent. In 1985, the one-firm firms relied almost exclusively on hiring "from the bottom." They resisted lateral hiring as unnecessary and risky to the firm's "fabric." But, as mentioned, things have changed dramatically.

One key feature still common to most one-firm firms is that the core (if no longer exclusive) strategy is to "grow their own" young talent. Professionals hired directly from school invariably have the strongest emotional ties to each other and to the firm, and they are the ones who find it hardest to abandon ship. Another advantage of focusing on young hires is a nimble, energetic army of people who are generally more willing to embrace the core teamwork culture and core values than are older lateral hires.

Many warlord firms have reduced or eliminated entry-level recruiting, purportedly because of the short-term cost of hiring and training such people. They prefer to hire laterally from other firms, to avoid the costs of investing in junior people.

> **One key feature still common to most one-firm firms is that the core (if no longer exclusive) strategy is to "grow their own" young talent.**

Such firms are sending two uncongenial messages: The people we hire are fungible, and there is nothing special about us. As a result, they fail to develop the loyalty and cohesiveness needed during periods of both prosperity and stress.

ALUMNI MANAGEMENT

One of the keys to the one-firm firm model is the vigorous enforcement of high standards for progression within the firm. This means that a relatively small percentage of those hired are actually promoted through the ranks. For that reason, the rates of nominal turnover in one-firm firms may not differ from those of other firms. However, one of the hallmarks of the model is that people who leave one-firm firms do so with great pride and loyalty, often becoming a source of business referrals for the firm.

Turnover among junior (and even senior) people has become a fact of life in all professions. In the 1980s, Latham learned that it made all the difference in the world whether people left feeling neglected or badly treated or as proud advocates of the firm.

Up to that point, Latham had ferociously concentrated on hiring, training, indoctrinating, and holding on to talent. In that environment, a lawyer leaving the firm to do something else was regarded as a failure rather than an opportunity. The pejorative term "attrition" was applied to these sad events. As a result, the firm often treated the departing lawyer as if he or she was a defector.

In retrospect, the firm lost millions of dollars in potential business because it mismanaged relationships with those who left. As Latham matured as an organization, it changed its practices to honor and cultivate the friendship of the people who leave the firm.

> **One of the hallmarks of the model is that people who leave one-firm firms do so with great pride and loyalty, often becoming a source of business referrals for the firm.**

In the mid-1990s, Latham calculated how much of then-current business came directly or indirectly from alums. The figure was approaching 50 percent. And it was great business —name-brand clients, often premium rates, quicker bill collection, pleasant dealings, and so on. Moreover, the clients benefited because the alums had a special feel for the firm, including knowledge of strengths and weaknesses. In some cases, alternative risk/reward billing arrangements could be worked out because of the built-in trust factor.

At all of the one-firm firms, the loyalty of alumni is a key competitive weapon. A leader in a one-firm firm said, "One of the managing partners of a competing firm once told me, 'The thing that strikes fear in our hearts is when one of your alums ends up as one of our clients—the loyalty is beyond our understanding and usually means it's just a matter of time before you guys have your nose under the tent.'"

THE ROLE OF **LATERAL HIRING**

Prior to the 1980s, firms entered new markets cautiously by redeploying existing talent. But affairs and clients began to move quickly, and markets have shifted much more rapidly in the years since then. Accordingly, most of the one-firm firms have expanded their use of lateral (experienced senior) hires. To wait for inside talent to develop was to risk missing the boat.

> **The lateral must understand that he or she is joining a firm with an established ideology. "If you don't like this ideology," the clear message is sent, "don't think of joining us."**

In addition, firms in every profession started to open offices in new geographic markets. Early attempts to staff new offices solely with partners from existing offices were unsuccessful. As a result, expanding firms began to cherry-pick talented, experienced people from outside the firm.

Most firms moved cautiously, bringing in only individuals and small groups and avoiding large-scale mergers. The key has been to make sure that when new laterals join the firm, they know what they are buying into. The lateral must understand that he or she is joining a firm with an established ideology. "If you don't like this ideology," the clear message is sent, "don't think of joining us."

Surprising to many outsiders, one-firm firms have found that many laterals come to the firm to benefit from good management; that is, to be managed. They know about the firm's reputation for effective management and team-based approaches, and they often come from poorly run firms. Often, not always, they are the most fervent supporters of teamwork, management, and cohesive action in their new organization.

Lateral hiring, now a competitive necessity, remains a double-edged sword for a one-firm firm. On the one hand, careful lateral hiring provides rich work opportunities for the "homegrowns." Also, laterals can help the firm challenge its settled view of itself. Done well, laterals can bring a new air of dynamism and creativity to a firm.

On the other hand, lateral hiring is management intensive. The bottom line is that a disciplined lateral program, anathema not very long ago, can strengthen a one-firm firm. A poorly managed program will tend to pull the firm apart.

THE ROLE OF **COMPENSATION SCHEMES**

The one-firm firms have largely avoided the stampede toward individual-based (or profit-center-based) reward schemes. However, since 1985 most one-firm firms have gradually expanded the individual component of their reward scheme (in fact if not in rhetoric) and have increased the total

> **The one-firm firms have largely avoided the stampede toward individual-based (or profit-center-based) reward schemes.**

compensation ratio between the highest-paid members and the lowest-paid members.

At Latham, until 1993 the long-term compensation element was essentially lockstep, driven mainly by seniority. Under cover of the early 1990s recession, this system was changed. Management's considered view was that the firm could not operate successfully in the emerging marketplace without providing more incentive for short- and long-term individual performance, particularly on the business development front.

Jack Walker reports that this was the hardest decision he had to make during his tenure as managing partner because of the obvious risk to the firm's "fabric." But because the change was sold and accepted as fundamentally respectful of the firm's ideology and shared values—not as a scuttling of them—it turned out to be a successful move. Since that change, the percentage of Latham partners hustling and producing business of substance has dramatically grown.

Most one-firm firms run judgment-based compensation schemes (with a studied avoidance of formulas). As always, the key to successful functioning of the system is agreement on values and ideology. This is because a successful compensation system requires trust: The members must believe that the compensation decisions are made by colleagues who have the firm's best interest as their only agenda.

> **Most one-firm firms run judgment-based compensation schemes (with a studied avoidance of formulas). As always, the key to successful functioning of the system is agreement on values and ideology.**

REVIEW: THE IMPORTANCE OF **TRUST AND LOYALTY**

There are many reasons why institutional trust and loyalty are important in a professional business, but three are worth stressing immediately.

First, clients of a one-firm firm have, as a practical matter, access

to all the resources of the firm. Individual members, rewarded through the overall success of the enterprise, are more
comfortable bringing in other parts of the firm to both win
and serve clients with complex multidisciplinary or multi-
jurisdictional matters.

Clients are generally better served than they would be by
a firm of solos or silos. Clients respond positively when individual members support (and, especially, do not undermine)
their colleagues. One-firm firms are good at both internal and
external relationships.

In firms that emphasize the use of credit and compensation systems to motivate (and placate) individual members, client service
across disciplines and geography will often suffer. Sophisticated
clients may cherry-pick great individual professionals or small
practice teams from such firms but will rarely depend on them
for complex work across boundaries. Warlord firms tend to excel
at transactions, not relationships across boundaries.

Second, as we have seen, the stewardship approach that
one-firm firms take toward their recruits (selectivity, training, high standards), when done well, can lead to great
alumni loyalty. One-firm firms do not necessarily have lower
levels of turnover, but former employees often leave as loyal
advocates of the firm, because of the way they were treated
when they were there. Employees of warlord firms do not
always feel this way. This can have a significant impact on
future revenues.

Third, trust and loyalty give a professional service
firm a better chance of surviv-
ing market downturns. The test
of a firm is not how it does in
good times, but rather how it
responds to roadblocks, stum-
bles, and both major and minor
problems.

> **One-firm firms do not
> necessarily have lower
> levels of turnover, but
> former employees
> often leave as loyal
> advocates of the firm.**

On such (inevitable) occasions, members of a loyalty-based firm will pull together, and they will take pride and pleasure in doing so.

In professional businesses with a free-agent climate, seemingly successful firms can and have disintegrated almost overnight. At the first sign of weakness, the strongest members of free-agent firms often feel that the sensible personal strategy is to build and cling to their personal client base and reputation.

At the very time when leadership is most needed, it is difficult to get the best people to work for the good of the firm. As firms grow weaker, the key members clutch ever more tightly to their client work and the firm flounders. Those who can, run for the door. It is not easy to reverse this spiral.

Many professional service firms are currently engaging in activities that undermine loyalty and create fault lines, including:

- Growing for growth's sake, by incoherently adding laterals and merging

- Expanding into unconnected practice areas and markets

- Hiring primarily semi-experienced lateral associates rather than hiring and training entry-level applicants

- Eliminating social and partner/officer meetings as a cost-cutting measure

- "Pulling up the ladder" to partner or owner status and establishing complex membership hierarchies, including non-equity levels, not to serve clients but to relieve inside pain

> **At the first sign of weakness, the strongest members of free-agent firms cling to their personal client base and reputation.**

- Obsessing about the short-term bottom line: treating financial success as the goal rather than as a by-product of a well-run firm

Joseph Heyison offers an interesting explanation of why such actions are common. Consider, he suggests, looking at the issue from the perspective of a powerful rainmaker in a professional service firm.

The bottom-line question is whether a rainmaker is better off supporting a warlord model and developing a strong portable practice that can be moved to another firm if the current firm suddenly gets into trouble. He notes that, while many firms have gone under in downturns, few rainmakers have.

Heyison's special insight is that firms compete not only for clients and junior staff, but also for rainmakers, and much of what we can see in the evolution of firms can best be understood in terms of that competition. This reasoning may indeed explain why some warlord firms (if staffed with truly skilled warlords) do well, at least in the short run.

THE STRESS OF **BOOM TIMES ON ONE-FIRM FIRMS**

Brian Sommer, a former Accenture partner, points out on his blog (*www.servicessafari.com*), in a posting called "The Lessons of Andersen," that too much individual incentive can lead firms into trouble in boom times as well as bad times:

"Great firms don't let their partners sell inappropriate work. They have a quality control process that prevents this. They utilize partners from different geographies, industries, etc., to do these quality control checks so that no one, in a position of career determination, can influence whether the work is sold and how it is structured.

"Great firms have a formalized approval process. Great firms protect their reputation as they realize that their brand is their number one asset. Great firms also pay all people in a relatively uniform way.

> **Too much individual incentive can lead firms into trouble in boom times as well as bad times.**

"Lone wolf selling and delivery, to get the biggest pile of money at the end of the year, drives way too many bad deals."

Jonathan Knee, in a review of his experiences working in investment banking (*The Accidental Investment Banker*), also points out that temptations can exist when a boom market allows firms to achieve rapid volume increases by relaxing their hiring or other quality standards. Management must be disciplined—must know how to say no—in prosperous times as well as in down times.

Our observation from watching one-firm firms over twenty years confirms Knee's observations. In highly prosperous periods, productive partners grow impatient with management's reluctance, for example, to hire hastily in order to staff all of their new production, or to promote their favorite, busiest partner candidates.

In busy times there is also a temptation to let investments such as training take a back seat to getting the work out the door. Only adherence to the firm's principles and values prevents opportunistic behavior that may have short-term benefits but long-term adverse consequences.

Rainmakers, who are always stressed but are even more so in boom times, often have little patience with the one-firm firm business disciplines. They are characteristically insecure about whether it will rain tomorrow for them. This insecurity compels them to hustle for new business.

They are also likely to compare their compensation with that of the leading rainmakers in the warlord firms. When they feel that they are not at the very top of their peer group, they often find it hard to trust in the future. This is especially true of members who did not "grow up" with the firm. It takes time to develop both loyalty and a long-term view.

> **Management must be disciplined—must know how to say no—in prosperous times as well as in down times.**

Managers of one-firm firms earn their money during these times. It is tempting to relax the disciplines in boom times, but boom times always recede and the bad calls always come back to haunt us.

SUMMARY

As we have tried to report, the five named one-firm firms are both similar to and different from what they were in 1985. Changes have happened in these firms, but they have been managed within a (mostly) coherent ideological framework.

Some specific one-firm firm practices have changed with positive effect, and some experimental moves away from the one-firm firm system were mistakes.

These firms may appear to lack the pure commitment to the ideals described in 1985, but they are still distinguished by their deep commitment to a teamwork approach.

So it may be fair to say that the 1985 profile of the one-firm firms left out one important item: flexibility, and the willingness to experiment and change *within* the firm's value system.

One-firm firms are known for their attention to what warlord firms would pejoratively characterize as "soft values."

If our experience since 1985 tells us anything, it is that this attention—balanced of course with high standards—can really pay off in terms of producing the kind of internal loyalties—and energy—necessary for long-term success.

CHAPTER SIXTEEN

Managing the
Multidimensional Organization

The previous chapter argued that more can be accomplished when firms are internally collaborative. However, as firms grow and become more diverse and complex, achieving collaboration across boundaries becomes more difficult. This chapter, coauthored with Patrick J. McKenna, explores some of the issues.

Professional businesses today are structurally complex organizations with many senior people overburdened by time-consuming and often conflicting roles. The organization is frequently divided into:

- Geographic markets or offices

- Product line/service offerings

- Industry (or client sector) groups

- Key account teams

- Division or departments

- Committees (recruitment, training)

> **Professional businesses today are structurally complex organizations with many senior people overburdened by time-consuming and often conflicting roles.**

• Task forces or project teams (service innovation, new offerings)

Each of these organizational groupings can, and does, intersect with duplicated missions, overlapping membership, and common resource pools to draw upon.

In many firms, it's not at all clear for what each of these groupings is responsible, nor how their activities should be coordinated and evaluated. A key player can be involved in multiple groups and spend an inordinate amount of time in meetings. The way professional businesses organize and manage has not kept up with their increasing complexity. Eventually, this will significantly impede their continuing success.

Not only do modern companies have more "types" of organizational groupings than in the past, but these groups now have broader responsibilities than the simple "generate and serve clients" goals of the past. To survive and flourish, individual groups within today's organizations must be accountable for client loyalty, knowledge transfer, development of their people (junior and senior), and many other "balanced scorecard" items.

To make it all worse, many of these groups are composed of people who, because of geographic dispersion, do not see each other regularly face-to-face. They have to operate as members of a "virtual" organization. Many would not even recognize some of the people in their own operating groups, with whom they have to interact regularly.

As Marcel Goldstein, of the global public relations firm Ogilvy, wrote to us:

"The modern-day professional business lacks much formal structure, at least when compared with manufacturers, government agencies, and other organizations. This is a great asset, as it allows the flexibility, creativity, and autonomy necessary to adapt to client

> **The way professional businesses organize and manage has not kept up with their increasing complexity.**

needs. It can have a darker side though: inefficiency, confusion, and process breakdowns.

"In many professions, clients are demanding cross-practice cooperation. But do we have the right structures and personal skill sets to successfully manage the integration of specialty expertise? The highly matrixed professional business turns downright chaotic during times of great change: acquisitions/mergers; technology disruptions; and transitions to integrated, cross-functional service delivery.

"We need structures that don't squash flexibility and creativity but minimize inefficiency and confusion. We need help building the personal skill sets needed to manage ourselves and each other in these environments, especially during times of great change."

EXAMINE **STRUCTURE, PROCESS,** AND **PEOPLE**

The solution for an individual firm must always address three perspectives in any organizational review: *structure* (how we are formally organized); *processes* (how different types of decisions are to be made and how conflicts and trade-offs are to be resolved); and *people* (appointing the right individuals to play the complex roles that will make it all work).

No one dimension will solve the problem: all three must be examined. However, the importance of these three elements in the solution is first, people; then processes; then structure.

CHOOSE THE **RIGHT GROUP LEADERS**

Many organizations believe that selecting the right leaders (and having enough of them) is more important than structure or process.

Peter Kalis, managing partner of Kirkpatrick & Lockhart,

> No one dimension will solve the problem: all three must be examined. However, the importance of these three elements in the solution is first, people; then processes; then structure.

states the view forcefully: "Structure and process—while as essential to a firm as a skeleton and a nervous system are to a human—are prone to ossification and thus are fundamentally at war with the dynamism of the marketplace. People, on the other hand, are not. We try to elevate the empowerment of our people over the organizational niceties of structure and process except to the extent that those structural and process features work to empower our people."

Choosing the right people for leadership positions was always important, but is even more critical in complex organizations. Consider just some of the (newly important?) skills that today's group leader probably must have:

- The ability (and interest) to motivate and influence people they never see in person

- The ability to delegate and trust others to manage important relationships

- The ability to play a "linking-pin" role, simultaneously thinking about the overall good of the firm while taking care of the needs of the units they are responsible for

- The ability to manage people who have core disciplines other than the one in which the leader was specifically trained

It has always been true that effective management requires a complex mix of social, interpersonal, psychological, political, and emotional skills on top of the high intelligence and technical skills necessary to rise to the top. As organizations become more complex, possession (and development) of these so-called soft skills

As organizations become more complex, possession (and development) of these so-called soft skills must play an ever-more-important role.

must play an ever-more-important role in influencing who is selected to perform managerial or leadership roles.

Unfortunately, such considerations do not always play a dominant role in selecting group leaders. It is a common syndrome that all initiatives (client team, industry, geographic, functional, etc.) are seen as important, so the same senior people always end up on all the committees, often based on considerations other than managerial aptitude or even orientation.

As a result, it is somewhat hit-and-miss as to whether the right people get selected for these roles, their mandate is clear, their performance as leaders gets discussed and evaluated, and whether they receive any assistance or guidance in learning how to perform their roles.

Not only does this hurt the organization by (possibly) leading to less effective team leadership, but it's not clear that it is wise to consume the limited time of valuable people by asking them to manage and/or get involved in everything. This is simple economics—a valuable resource should always be focused on its highest and best use.

ESTABLISH MANDATES FOR EACH GROUP

Even if you have an ideal structure, there will always be problems with coordinating cross-boundary resources and dealing with conflicting priorities. You cannot make all cross-boundary issues go away by simply redesigning the boundaries.

Beyond structure, companies must ensure that each group has a clear mission (or mandate) that is understood by those inside and outside the group. Many firms launch new business units, various committees, or project teams with ambiguous charters and then leave it to powerful (or not-so-powerful) group leaders

> This is simple economics—a valuable resource should always be focused on its highest and best use.

to determine through negotiations over time precisely how the groups will interact.

The case *for* doing this rests on the idea that internal competition is the inevitable result of shifting external market forces influencing each of the organization's groups differently and that a flexible approach to the responsibilities and interactions of groups is an efficient way of responding to these external market forces.

However, failing to discuss and resolve the issues of group responsibilities (and how groups will interact and resolve conflicts and trade-offs) rarely results in optimal outcomes.

Under such an approach, power rather than principle determines group goals and how groups will interact, and this leads to lesser performance. Resolution of conflicting goals and clear, agreed-upon guidelines for decision making over trade-off situations must be determined in advance.

Organizations must stop treating all groups alike, which many unfortunately do for administrative convenience. It is possible to use different types of groups for different things: lots of little teams for client-level relationships or one large central group for financial and administrative services.

A large, growing, and complex firm doesn't have to be (in fact, can't be) made up of units that have similar roles, look alike, have the same targets, and are managed in the same way. (See our book *First Among Equals*.)

In making all this work, it is better to stop thinking of permanent or semipermanent "departments" and to begin to use the language of "teams." Organizations work better when three components exist: people feel that they are volunteers, self-selected to join small, mission-oriented teams. Professional businesses

> **Organizations work better when three components exist: people feel that they are volunteers, self-selected to join small, mission-oriented teams.**

succeed most by designing their organizations from the bottom up—through the voluntary enthusiasm of individuals, who are then aggregated into teams which have a community and commonality of interest.

When it comes to doing strategy, a firm would be better off with a messy set of teams filled with enthusiasts than it would be with a logically correct set of groups filled with good citizens.

As Ben Johnson of Alston & Bird remarked, "Too many 'leaders' are afraid to create more energy than they can control. I tell people I'd rather have created more energy than I could control than not created any energy at all. Here's to structural complexity! Here's to dispersed leadership!"

On the other hand, it is also important that firms clarify the roles and responsibilities of group leaders and avoid the balkanization of the organization that can come from letting group leaders think that they are responsible only for their groups. Excessive use of profit centers is rarely a good idea for complex organizations.

CLARIFY AGREEMENTS WITHIN THE GROUPS

Whether you are managing a division, a key client team, or a limited-scope task force, every group needs to have a very clear understanding of what "team membership" implies. As a matter of practicality (although not, alas, reality in some firms) there also needs to be a limit on the number of teams one person can join (and the number of roles one person can play).

For teams to work, there need to be clear, explicit guidelines (even rules of engagement) that team members have agreed to observe. Clarifying team members' rights and obligations can go a long way toward becoming more efficient and effective. (Even as simple a rule as "You must do what you said you were

Professional businesses succeed most by designing their organizations from the bottom up.

going to do" would transform some organizations and save a lot of wasted meeting and planning time.)

If far-flung groups made up of many autonomous individuals are to make cohesive decisions over time, then it is necessary that the group members agree in advance the principles on which they will base their decisions—the guidelines the group members agree to follow. Only with such an agreement in place can a decentralized organization make consistent decisions.

Part of the solution, may involve thinking of (and formalizing) different levels of team membership. For example, levels of "team membership" might include (i) full decision rights—possible called Team Leadership, or (ii) right to be consulted—called team membership or (iii) right to be kept informed—called team affiliation. (These are examples only.)

RECOGNIZE SHIFTING **PRIORITIES** IN **STRUCTURAL DESIGN**

Structural changes alone will not resolve conflicting priorities and competing demands for resources, but structure does nevertheless matter. The evolution of professional-service firms over time suggests that some structural approaches do work better than others. Most successful global firms, in a broad array of professions, have tilted the importance of their different organizational "axes."

For some time, there has been a general trend to make the target client industry the most important (and organizationally powerful) grouping. This has been driven by clients repeatedly telling their vendors and providers that they had better get to know and understand the client's business.

> There has been a general trend to make the target client industry the most important (and organizationally powerful) grouping.

Next in authority and emphasis comes the specifically targeted client (or key account) team. Well-orchestrated client teams are the only answer to making seamless service across geography and product/service offerings a reality.

Third, and with increasingly *less* power and responsibility inside most organizations, are the traditional product or service-line groups built around a focused technical specialty or discipline. Companies need to have highly focused and skilled technical people, but few are still primarily organized that way.

Finally (and this is a huge revolution from the past), the trend has been to make geography the least important and powerful dimension of the complex matrix.

In the past, the office head (or country head in megafirms) was the source of all resources and the arbiter of last resort. Today, in many organizations, a geographic head may preside over a location whose people all belong to groups headed and "controlled" by a powerful leader located elsewhere.

This is not meant to denigrate the role of the geographic leader. As Bob Dell of Latham & Watkins points out, "Having the right leader in an office can be extremely effective in facilitating the success of all the other groups therein. There seems to be something about physical presence combined with a leader who is perceived as less biased toward any group that can be very powerful in resolving competing demands."

MOVING **FORWARD**

Regardless of the final design, it will be necessary to implement methods for the development of special managerial skills and competencies as well as new metrics that may give better indications of the organization's functioning and response to external forces or internal pressures.

It may also be necessary to design a process to get the organization to recommit to a clarified sense of purpose, values, and "rules of membership":— the principles and practices that people must follow to remain

Well-orchestrated client teams are the only answer to making seamless service across geography and product/service offerings a reality.

members in good standing of the organization. (See chapter 5, "What's Our Deal?")

Of course, to make any of this work, there is a need for key players to be willing to let other people decide some things even when they're not there—a situation which does not exist in many companies and firms!

This is not a throwaway line. To effect real change, organizations must not try to establish "theoretically correct" structures and processes but must have honest discussions among powerful players about the types and nature of the firm's group processes that would, in fact, be honored.

We have seen too many firms go through the motions of putting in place what appear to be sensible organizations, when everyone knows that certain key players will not adhere to the policies that have been adopted.

We're not idealists here—we recognize the realities of the need to accommodate personalities and special situations. But we also do not believe that progress is made by pretending or obtaining "false consent." That is why organizational solutions must be custom-designed for each firm and need to be the result of a comprehensive review, not, as is so frequently the case, the net result of an accumulation of a series of incremental changes driven by short-run pressures.

CHAPTER SEVENTEEN

The **Trouble** With **Lawyers**

This article was originally intended to be exclusively about why lawyers and law firms are different from other professions. It explores the underlying issues that can prevent a group of smart people from developing and executing a common strategy—the difficulties of 'putting it together."

After it originally appeared, I started getting comments from clients in other businesses such as consulting and financial services who told me that I had accurately described the culture and behavior of their professions.

If you are not a lawyer, you may want to skip this chapter. However, there may, indeed, be lessons for other types of firms here. The topics it examines (trust, values, intimacy and decision-making) are universal.

After spending 25 years saying that all professions are similar and can learn from each other, I'm now ready to make a concession: Law firms are different.

The ways of thinking and behaving that help lawyers excel in their profession may be the very things that limit what they can achieve as firms. Management challenges occur not in spite of lawyers' intelligence and training, but because of them.

Among the ways that legal training and practice keep lawyers from effectively functioning in groups are

- problems with trust

- difficulties with ideology, values, and principles

> The ways of thinking and behaving that help lawyers excel in their profession may be the very things that limit what they can achieve as firms.

- professional detachment

- and unusual approaches to decision making

If firms cannot overcome these inherent tendencies, they may not be able to deliver on the goals and strategies they say they pursue.

THE PROBLEM OF TRUST

Much current practice in firm governance, organization, and (not least) compensation comes from the fact that partners vigorously defend their rights to autonomy and individualism, well beyond what is common in other professions. There is nothing inherently wrong with that.

However, as major corporations consolidate their work among a smaller number of firms, domestically and internationally, they expect that firms will serve them with effective cross-office and cross-disciplinary teams. Firms are vigorously responding to this with a stampede of lateral hires, mergers, and acquisitions. Their goal is to create big organizations offering many disciplines, locations, and cultures.

The unanswered—actually, barely asked—question is whether these firms can shift from a managerial approach, based on partner autonomy, to new approaches that can create a well-coordinated set of team players. Is the tradition of autonomy at the heart of a partner's identity, or can it change?

The barely asked question is whether these firms can shift from an approach based on partner autonomy to new approaches that create a well coordinated set of team players.

In addition to fighting vigorously to preserve their autonomy, lawyers are professional skeptics: They are selected, trained, and hired to be pessimistic and to spot flaws. To protect their clients, they place the worst possible construction on the outcome of any idea or proposal, and on the motives, intentions, and likely behaviors of those they are dealing with. As Tony Sacker, my kind and gentle brother-in-law and a solicitor in the United Kingdom, says, "I am paid to have a nasty, suspicious mind."

Lawyers carry this view into their dealings with their own partners. It is hard to unbundle which is the cause and which is the effect, but the combination of a desire for autonomy and high levels of skepticism make most law firms *low-trust environments*.

Recently, I was advising a firm on its compensation system. They didn't like my recommendations. Finally, one of the partners said, "David, all your recommendations are based on the assumption that we trust each other and trust our executive or compensation committees. We don't. Give us a system that doesn't require us to trust each other!"

A former managing partner with whom I have discussed this says, "It's not that I don't trust my partners. They're good people, mostly. It's that I don't want to have to trust them. Why give up any degree of control over your own affairs if you don't have to?"

Actually, a low-trust environment has plenty of unfortunate consequences—and they are readily observable in many law firms.

Initiatives that depend on teamwork and joint efforts will rarely be implemented well, if at all. People may show up to a practice group meeting and help develop a joint plan, but they rarely feel mutually committed to or accountable for the group's decisions. When lawyers cannot depend on their colleagues to live up to commitments made in these meetings, they give themselves permission to have a similar attitude, and the situation spirals downward.

When a firm's prevailing atmosphere is one of competition, not collaboration, partners rarely make

> The combination of a desire for autonomy and high levels of skepticism make most law firms low-trust environment.

sacrifices for the good of the firm. For example, they will be reluctant to take on managerial roles that might require them to limit their full-time practices, for fear that their partners will not treat them equitably when the time comes for them to reenter full-time practice.

There is low tolerance for ceding power or influence to practice group or firm leadership. The result is that even in the largest firms, executive authority can be so severely limited as to be meaningless. Decisions are made slowly, if not avoided altogether.

Committees proliferate to address all topics, large and small. They are designed not only to ensure extensive participation, but also to put in place checks and balances intended to circumscribe the ability of any individual (or group) to decide anything on behalf of the firm. This may have the virtue of being democratic, but it is a primitive form of democracy that requires everyone to be involved in every decision. It both slows down decision making and unnecessarily distracts from other, more productive tasks.

There is a drive to seemingly objective formula-based compensation systems. These serve only to entice partners into gaming the system through hoarding work and bickering over origination credits in order to look good in the official statistics. Partners constantly ask, "What's in the compensation formula?" and they do only those things that are. As a result, many behaviors necessary for the firm's success cannot be enforced, because they are not in the formula. Firm leaders have bemoaned this situation for decades, but few have found a way to solve it.

> **Even in the largest firms, executive authority can be so severely limited as to be meaningless. Decisions are made slowly, if not avoided altogether.**

Most important, absence of trust may be a significant contributing factor to the extremely short-term orientations of many law firms. If partners don't believe the firm will remember or value their contributions to future success, why would they make any investment that they may not ultimately get credit for?

As one of my clients—a former managing partner at a high-profile firm—observed about many law firms he knew:

"Most partners were recognized and rewarded for being the smartest person in the class or the most accomplished. They have rarely experienced or understood the power of succeeding as part of a larger group or team. Their focus tends to be selfish and self-serving, even narcissistic. The result is that the firm resources are squandered and poorly used, clients don't get the best lawyers assigned to their files, and firms are less profitable. This selfishness also leads to a shortsighted approach to decision making that inhibits long-range success because investments of time or money that don't yield immediate results are rarely made."

SKEPTICISM ABOUT **IDEOLOGY, VALUES, AND PRINCIPLES**

The single biggest source of trust in an organization occurs when everyone can be depended upon to act in accordance with a commonly held, strictly observed set of principles. Examples of such principles are "Our clients' interests always come first; if we serve our clients well, our own success will follow" and "We have no room for those who put their personal interests ahead of the interests of the firm and its clients." (Both of these, by the way, are from Goldman Sachs—see chapter 15.)

It is important to note that commercial benefits do not come simply from believing in or encouraging these principles but from actually achieving an organization where partner behavior is always consistent with them. When this is the case, less time is wasted in internal negotiations

> **The single biggest source of trust in an organization occurs when everyone can be depended upon to act in accordance with a commonly held, strictly observed set of principles.**

and posturing, strategies are implemented, and true team-work results. Partners allow others to make decisions on their behalf or refer work to each other across the boundaries of practice groups and location because they can be confident that the other person will make decisions using the same values and principles that they would themselves use.

Law firms appear unable to achieve this level of ideological consistency. They will buy into principles—firms can have very high ideals as long as they remain ideals—but they have difficulty with the concept of enforcement. Firms are seemingly willing to adopt strategies and statements of values and mission, but are usually unwilling to specify what the penalty would be for noncompliance. Not surprisingly, that rarely results in effective implementation.

There is a reason for this. As a partner in an eminent U.S. firm points out, "Lawyers raised in the common-law tradition are trained to have a deep suspicion of overarching principles. The essence of the common-law approach is that decisions are made incrementally, always leaving open the possibility that the next case could be treated completely differently."

In my consulting work I have repeatedly advocated a system of help and coaching for partners who fail to meet the firm's standards. If coaching fails to bring a partner up to the firm's standards after a fair and reasonable amount of time, the partner is asked to leave. This is, in fact, close to the system that firms employ with respect to partners who fail to hit financial targets such as billable hours.

However, the point I keep trying to make is that if a firm wishes to excel in other areas, such as client service, collaboration, or associate supervision, the same process should apply. The response is predictable. Most law firms say that the idea of tackling a rainmaker on these "soft" issues is unrealistic, idealistic, uncommercial, and

Law firms appear unable to achieve this level of ideological consistency.

suicidal. In vain I point out that these standards are what firms already preach in their client and recruiting brochures and claim as their values.

While a majority of firms will vote to proclaim standards, they will usually not vote to enforce them. Indeed, the signs are that they vigorously prefer the opposite: Law firms have a proliferating plethora of rules, not functioning principles, because they don't or won't trust that their partners will adhere to the values, standards, and principles that they agreed upon. So firms end up with a mishmash of bureaucratic red tape in the hope that mandatory processes will achieve compliance when adherence to common values does not.

PROFESSIONAL **DETACHMENT**

In their legal training, lawyers are encouraged to be dispassionate. They have been schooled to leave their personal feelings at home. One lawyer told a consultant friend of mine that when he hung up his jacket on the back of his door in the morning, with it went his personality, both of which he put on at the end of the day as he left the office.

As many researchers have shown, lawyers score very low in the areas of intimacy skills and sociability. They tend to prefer role-to-role interactions with people, inside and outside the firm, rather than eagerly seeking out person-to-person connections. This doesn't mean they don't like people. It just means that, statistically speaking, lawyers prefer focusing on the job at hand rather than investing in relationships with those they are working with (other partners or associates) or for (clients).

This can have unfortunate, if unintended, consequences.

> **Lawyers prefer focusing on the job at hand rather than investing in relationships with those they are working with (other partners or associates) or for (clients).**

Consider this e-mail, which I recently received from Marein Smits, a Dutch lawyer:

"At your recent seminar you made fun of me because I laughed at the idea of being genuinely interested in the industry and business of the people who are my clients. Rightly so: My laughing was cynical… The first thing you learn when you become a lawyer is not to care. The legally sound judgment, the intellectual sparkle; that is what counts. The personal, the emotional, what is right: Throw it away, because it will taint your professionalism. 'Do not get involved' is the credo."

A major rainmaker once pointed out to me, "I can't convince my partners that this is all about human beings, that you market most successfully by showing an interest in the client as a person. My partners really don't want to express that level of intimacy with anyone at work." This lack of intimacy affects not only marketing and client relations, but also the way in which partners deal with each other and how firms are managed.

Rather than describing a highly interpersonal approach to coaching and helping each other succeed, the term "management" has come in many firms to mean a cold, detached, analytical approach to business. Financial scorecards are put in place, and everyone is told (implicitly or explicitly), "Here's what you will be measured on; see you at the end of the year!" They are not helped to achieve, merely rewarded if they do, and they live in fear of what might happen if they do not. This can achieve the goal of getting everyone to work harder, but it comes at a significant price in terms of partner morale and cohesion. Help, teamwork, and mutual support are often absent, since they depend on personal interactions. Instead, there is a system of measures and rewards.

In these days of ever-accelerating partner and associate mobility, a firm tied together only by measures and rewards will be inherently unstable.

While this approach is the one preferred by many partners (and many firms) it inherently limits creation of a strategically responsive organization. In these days of ever-accelerating partner and associate mobility, a firm tied together only by measures and rewards will be inherently unstable.

There are signs that a few firms are recognizing the importance of this issue. Says one managing partner: "The idea has slowly taken hold in our firm that one should deal with people as people, show warmth and empathy, and build personal relationships with others in the firm… My leadership style has evolved over the years from trying to be comprehensive and logical to relying more on developing personal rapport and trying to motivate people." This insight might be gaining ground. But the behavior inside many law firms has yet to catch up.

APPROACHES TO **DECISION MAKING**

When it comes to discussing their firms' affairs, lawyers have peculiar ways of conducting discussions and arriving (or not arriving) at decisions. The essence of lawyers' training and daily practice is to contest with other lawyers. While winning arguments against nonlawyers (such as consultants like me) is mere sport, winning them against other lawyers is a deadly serious business—a challenge to their core ability.

In a room full of lawyers, any idea, no matter how brilliant, will be instantly attacked. Lawyers are expert loophole finders, trained to find counterexamples of or exceptions to any proposition. Accordingly, within a short time, most ideas, no matter who initiates them, will be destroyed, dismissed, or postponed for future examination.

Frequently, this leads managing partners, committee chairs, and practice group leaders to substantially overinvest in decision making. They want to be armed

> **In a room full of lawyers, any idea, no matter how brilliant, will be instantly attacked.**

in advance with a lengthy memo about every decision so they can dump it in the lap of the complainer as part of fending off the attack.

Another common management strategy is to keep all proposals ambiguous, so that there is nothing specific to be attacked. As a result, law firms have a remarkable propensity for half measures, launching poorly specified programs with minimal chances of success. A common law firm dialogue is as follows: Let's have client service teams! (All agree.) What do we mean by such teams? (We don't want to say yet.) What shall their responsibilities be? (That's to be worked out.) What are the obligations of team members to each other? (We'll let them figure it out.) Combine all this with the obligation to resolve issues through committees, and you have a recipe for business constipation.

This is not necessarily a problem for lawyers. My own attorney pointed out, "You are taught in law school that there are no right answers. We are actively trained to be nondecisive and are comfortable with a lack of closure."

When lawyers reason with each other, the primary objectives are not necessarily logic, consistency, reasonableness, or fairness. In their professional practice, whether in trial or deal-making, many lawyers are more frequently rewarded for persuasiveness, rhetoric, verbal agility, and point scoring. These habits of a professional lifetime readily spill over into internal firm discussions.

Lawyers also have a strange view of the concept of risk. In any other business, an idea that was likely to work much of the time would be eagerly explored. This is not necessarily the case with lawyers. If one partner says, "This works in the vast majority of cases," you can be sure that another will say, "Maybe, but I can construct a

> **When lawyers reason with each other, the primary objectives are not necessarily logic, consistency, reasonableness, or fairness.**

hypothetical scenario where it will fail to work. That makes it risky." Probabilities do not seem to influence the discussion, only possibilities. There is no greater condemnation in legal discourse than to describe something as risky. Contracts, deals, and court cases must be bulletproof, not risky.

In other businesses, innovative thinking and action are considered a primary requirement for success. Companies eagerly search for strategic ideas and initiatives that their competitors have not discovered.

Lawyers are usually different. Presented with a new business idea, the first thing they ask is, "Which other law firms are doing this?" Unless it can be shown that the idea has been implemented by other law firms, lawyers are skeptical about whether the idea applies to their world. If everyone has these problems, they can't be so bad, the thinking goes. As long as we are no worse than anyone else, we don't need to change! It's hardly a recipe for a strategic advantage.

WHAT **CAN BE DONE?**

If lawyers deal with each other so poorly, why do they do so well financially? My answer is only partly humorous: The greatest advantage lawyers have is that they compete only with other lawyers. If everyone else does things equally poorly, and clients and recruits find little variation between firms, even the most egregious behavior will not lead to a competitive disadvantage.

A persuasive case can be made that lawyers will not change, because times are good and partners (and associates, for that matter) earn a lot of money. However, the question always arises as to how the money is being made. Many law firms have discovered that you can truly make a lot of money if you work everybody very, very hard and really slash your costs and don't care about

> **If lawyers deal with each other so poorly, why do they do so well financially?**

how people—partners, associates, or staff—feel about their work lives.

While that's one approach to riches, it can be shown (as in my book *Practice What You Preach*) that it is not the best or most sustainable approach to riches. "Let's succeed by working more hours with ever-decreasing amounts of support" is not the most sophisticated piece of business thinking I have ever heard. The answer, for firms that choose to pursue it, lies not in ever-more-sophisticated (and tough) business management tools, but in a head-on confrontation with the issues of trust, values, interpersonal behavior, and decision-making logic that I have explored here.

If firms are to deliver on the visions they have set for themselves, they must address such issues as what behavior partners have a right to expect from each other, what the real minimum standards and values are, and how common values and standards can actually be attained, not just preached.

Unless law firms undergo a cultural revolution, not just minor changes, most will not be able to achieve their ambitions. Dysfunctional behavior by partners, currently not only tolerated but vigorously celebrated, will prevent firms from functioning as they desire.

There is some hope, because what have been reported here are common tendencies, not ironclad laws. There are firms that are exceptional, singular counterexamples to the propositions explored here, and they are tackling head-on the core issues of culture, trust, and partner behavior. On the other hand, many other firms are doing the very things that will prevent them from creating the truly collaborative organizations their lawyers say that they want.

> **"Let's succeed by working more hours with ever-decreasing amounts of support" is not the most sophisticated piece of business thinking I have ever heard.**

One of the central things we know about trust and collaboration is that they come mostly from repeated interactions between people who have not only a history together, but also the certainty of a future together. Trust comes from relationships and the expectation of continuing relationships. Over time, as they interact with each other, they as partners, practice groups, and offices may actually come to trust each other.

Unfortunately, in many of today's firms that have been cobbled together from lateral hires and newly merged practices, the personal history that forms the basis of trust is often missing, as is the confidence that everyone will be practicing together for a long time. In many firms, even solidly successful partners live in fear that they will be among the next group of partners to be "let go."

In such an environment, the natural evolution of trust may be difficult, if not impossible. Instead, what firms need, literally, is a constitutional convention where their lawyers draft the explicit, basic law that is going to govern their firms—the precise behaviors, rules, and principles that will determine what partners have a right to expect from each other.

When thought of as aspirations (which is usually the case), firms' values are usually explicitly articulated and remarkably similar. However, if a value is seen as a minimum standard of behavior that all members agree to live by, then the true values remain ambiguous in most firms and vary immensely among firms.

Firms have historically flourished without constitutions that spell out minimum partner behaviors. For many, profits and revenues keep rising. What then will be the force that might create the need for change? Most likely, it will be client pressure on firms to act as firms—delivering seamless service, practice areas that have depth (and not just a collection of individualistic stars), and true, cross-boundary teamwork.

The answer lies in a head-on confrontation with the issues of trust, values, interpersonal behavior, and decision-making logic.

Many firms have collections of great lawyers. The time may be coming when clients will expect them to go beyond this and become effective organizations. Without a prior, explicit agreement on minimum standards, and the resolve to enforce them, many law firms will not function well as firms but will remain what they are today: bands of warlords, each with his or her followers, ruling over a group of cowed citizens and acting in temporary alliance—until a better opportunity comes along.

CHAPTER EIGHTEEN

The **Chief Executive's** Speech

In case your chief executive needs a speech, here's one I wrote ten years ago for the leader of a large, national professional firm who asked me what he should say upon his election to the role.

Our firm, like our best competitors, is aiming at familiar goals. We want not only to be the best, but to be perceived by our clients as such. We want to be innovative, and at the frontier of identifying and responding to the needs of both global and middle market clients. We want to capitalize on the latest technological developments. We want to give our clients an unmatched level of client service.

We also want our firm to be a place that provides professional fulfillment and personal growth opportunities for each and every one of our partners, non-partners, and staff. We believe that doing these things will make us one of the most profitable firms in our profession.

These goals are not unique to us. Our best competitors almost certainly have similar, if not identical goals. If we are to outperform

Our firm is aiming at familiar goals. These goals are not unique to us.

them, we don't need a better vision, but a better approach to making it happen. We will succeed not by aiming at different targets than our best competitors do, but by devising better ways to reach those same targets. We must develop and adhere strictly to sound philosophies: ways of doing business, ways of dealing with our clients, our people, and each other.

In sum, we must agree not on our destination, but on a way of conducting our affairs. We must design systems to ensure that we are living up to our principles.

In preparing these thoughts, I have not attempted to picture what the firm will look like in five or ten years. Rather, I have tried to convey the philosophies I hold about how we should behave as individuals and as a firm. If we follow these principles, we will achieve our goals. If we do not, then we will fail.

I have also avoided being inspirational. These are the principles I both live by, and intend to apply in executing my responsibilities. By sharing these beliefs with you, I am making you a promise that these are the principles I will operate by—and I expect you to hold me accountable for them. If I depart from these principles, let me know—in person, in a letter, or even, if necessary, in an anonymous note. But let me know!

I do not expect that all of you will necessarily agree with everything I have to say. That's OK, and we should talk about it. But what is here is what I truly believe. You have the right to know where I am coming from, and how I am likely to react when you ask for my views on issues as they arise.

For better or for worse, then, this is what I believe.

> You have the right to know where I am coming from, and how I am likely to react. For better or for worse, then, this is what I believe.

ON THE **ROLE OF THE PARTNER**

Since clients hire people, not firms, our success will be built a partner at a time. That means that what really matters is not "firm strategies" but personal career-development strategies for each partner. If, and only if, each partner is finding some way to make himself/herself more valuable in the marketplace each year, then the firm will succeed.

In turn, this means that the role of the firm is to help each individual grow as a professional. The firm exists to help its people succeed, not the other way round. However, it also means that the firm has the right to expect each person to develop a personal development plan, and to hold that person accountable for the execution of that plan.

In this profession, the need for personal development is life-long. The minute you begin to cruise, to rely on skills learned last year, that's the moment you begin your decline. All of us, from the thirty-year-olds to the sixty-year olds must constantly ask, "What new skills can I acquire?" And the firm has the right to ask that same question of you.

My experience has taught me that success comes not to those who swing for the fences every time at bat, but to those who commit themselves to a continuous program of constant improvement, base hit by base hit.

There are many ways to make yourself more valuable in the market: intellectual leadership, better client counseling skills, a greater ability to run large projects, and so on. But one stands above all else: specialized industry knowledge. Regardless of your discipline, and your command of it, each and every partner should have in-depth, up-to-date knowledge in one or more industries, so that clients perceive you as having a special interest in them and their business. There is no better way, in my view, for each of us to succeed than for every one of us to declare a specific industry specialization.

Senior professionals, in my opinion, have five key responsibilities, for which they should expect to be held accountable.

> **The firm exists to help its people succeed, not the other way round.**

First, and foremost, all individuals and every team must satisfy their clients, and we should be vigorous in establishing processes which ensure this is happening.

Second, those running client assignments or engagements must be responsible for building skills in themselves and others, thereby adding to the human capital of the firm. We sell skill and talent, not time. We should devise tracking mechanisms to allow partners to see how well they are fulfilling this responsibility.

Third, those in charge of assignments have a responsibility to contribute to the economic success of the firm by running their engagements profitably, and constantly seeking out ways to improve the economics of their work. We must learn to use our resources efficiently, and that means we should be vigorous in tracking how well we are using them. Each senior person owes us all the responsibility of managing well not only our revenues, but the costs to the firm in delivering our services.

Fourth, everyone should participate *in some way* to developing our business by attracting and winning quality new work and new clients that allow us to stretch, learn, and grow.

This does not mean just getting *more* business, it means getting *better* business. We should establish procedures to judge not only the volume of our business, but its caliber. Our goal should not be to chase any and all new business, but to get more than our fair share of the best business. Our goal is to be recognized as being unequivocally the best, not the biggest. When you hear from me, expect to hear more questions about the quality and nature of what you're doing than how much you are doing.

In the pursuit of quality new business, everyone should play a role. Some will do it directly through selling and proposal efforts, others through writing articles, others through deep involvement with existing clients and their affairs. But each one of us

> **Our goal should not be to chase any and all new business, but to get more than our fair share of the best business.**

must play some part in the improvement of our practice through attracting interesting, challenging new work.

Last, but not least, every person has a responsibility to contribute to the success of others. We need to act as a partnership, and not a collection of solo operators (or independent offices) trading under the same brand name. If the firm is to achieve its goal of helping each person succeed, then we must help each other. Each person should be able, each year, to point to some specific contribution to the success of others. This may be bringing in work for others to do, developing methodologies or technical ideas that others can use, or transferring skills to others through coaching. But one way or another, we each must do something if we are to be a firm.

Contributing to the success of others should (and will be) a criterion applied in judging the success of practice units, offices, and disciplines. Any group that focuses only on its own results and does not help others will not be judged a success.

ON **ACCOUNTABILITY**

If someone has accepted a responsibility, and agreed upon a goal, then we should get out of his or her way and let the individual do it. None of us should wait to be told what to do, or how to do it. Micromanagement kills initiative, judgment and creativity.

That doesn't mean abdication. It means that, after establishing clear goals and accountability measures, we should turn people loose to pursue those goals, with the freedom and responsibility to figure out how to get things done.

ON **EVALUATIONS**

In judging performance, we must be thorough in conducting performance appraisals that focus on non-financial as well as financial objectives, and we must vigorously

Any group that focuses only on its own results and does not help others will not be judged a success.

ensure that each person receives regular in-depth feedback, assistance and coaching on performance. Our reward systems must derive from these regular, thorough and constructive counseling approaches and must never be a substitute for them.

ON **MANAGEMENT**

Our firm has no room for managers who spend their time on administration, play cop or boss, or use the job for their own reward and glory. The job of a manager is to help other people succeed. It is a responsibility, not a reward. We must not glorify those who occupy managerial positions, but choose the person most skilled at managerial duties, and keep them and reward them only if they perform the role well and make a difference to the performance of others.

Managers should be deeply involved in client affairs, not necessarily by being the lead partner on their own engagements, but by spending significant time on client relations, by being a practical source of help on other partners' assignments, and by participating in other people's business development activities.

Managers should also be deeply involved with the activities of the people in the group they are responsible for. They should be available to resolve issues, form teams, provide assistance and make it easier for other people to focus on their clients. Managers should be hassle absorbers, not hassle creators.

> **We must not glorify those who occupy managerial positions, but choose the person most skilled at managerial duties, and keep them and reward them only if they perform the role well and make a difference to the performance of others.**

All of us must be willing to be accountable for performing our respective roles well. If our people are to be held accountable for their performance (financial and non-financial), the same must be true of those asked to accept managerial responsibilities.

ON CLIENTS AND **WHAT THEY WANT**

I believe that clients can make few distinctions on the technical capabilities of the best firms and, as a result, place great emphasis on the ability of the individual partner to enter their world, relate to them in their language, and talk to them about their business. We will never succeed by being technicians alone, no matter how high our level of technical skill. Clients want us to know their business. They want us to be interested in them.

ON **MY STYLE**

I like to be decisive. I have learned that we can live with a bad decision, but we are certain to be hurt by no decision. I am willing to take risks, and to encourage and reward risk taking. Call me on that if I depart from it.

I like to ask, "What new things have you tried lately?" Only by trying new things will we get better.

I like to be consultative. That doesn't mean unanimity, or even consensus. It means soliciting views, asking a lot of questions, and then deciding. I like to hear other people's opinions. Don't let me behave any other way.

I don't like to launch things that I'm not prepared to follow through on. If I'm involved in an initiative, expect me to monitor it carefully—and let me know if I don't. I don't make promises I can't keep; you should fire me if I don't live up to that promise.

I like to be straight and tell the truth, and I like to be told the truth. I want to hear the bad news, if there is any, and I want to hear it early enough for me to try to help and do something about it. Life's too short for politics and playing games.

I believe in extensive two-way communications between management and those they manage.

> I don't make promises I can't keep; you should fire me if I don't live up to that promise.

This will mean meeting with clients and employees frequent-ly. Keep me honest on this one, and let me know if what I'm doing is insufficient.

SUMMARY

That's not all I believe, but it's enough for now. I hope you found these thoughts interesting, and helpful. I hope you watch me carefully to ensure that I live by what I advocate.

If not, well then, you know what to do. Let me know!

CHAPTER NINETEEN

Passion, People, and Principles

So what have we learned about how to overcome the Fat Smoker syndrome? How does an individual or organization live up to its own highest standards, resisting temptation and keeping its eyes firmly fixed on the prize? A few of this book's key themes are identified and summarized here.

F or individuals and organizations to succeed—to get done what they know they should be doing—they need to possess three things: passion, a sincere interest in (and understanding of) people, and principles.

PASSION

As we have seen, drive and determination—passion—are the hallmarks of all successful individuals and businesses. Only where an (almost inexplicable) desire exists to achieve something new will people and institutions find the discipline to resist the short-term temptations to deviate from their chosen path.

> **For individuals and organizations to succeed—to get done what they know they should be doing—they need to possess three things: passion, a sincere interest in (and understanding of) people, and principles.**

This passion may be innate in some individuals. Others will require skilled, effective managers to elicit and channel their energy and enthusiasm. Indeed, since no organization is likely to be built on naturally self-sustaining dynamos alone, skilled managers acting like coaches are an essential requirement for success. You could conclude, as I do, that creating and channeling energy is the predominant if not sole requirement in what distinguishes a great manager from a barely competent one.

Give people just a goal, and little will be accomplished. Leave it to them to find self-discipline, and most will fail to sustain high intensity. But place them in an environment where they are well coached, with colleagues equally turned on, and—contrary to what cynics might believe—the overwhelming majority of people of all backgrounds and educational levels will respond with enthusiasm and commitment.

Sustained passion is a scarce, fragile phenomenon. It can be compromised by success itself (why try so hard when so much has been accomplished?), by variably enforced standards (why try so hard if others in the organization do not?), or by cynicism (why try so hard when we don't really care about what we do or those for whom we do it?)

But without it, little success can be had.

PEOPLE

Many of us come to realize, later than we should, that no matter what you want in life, what you want to obtain—riches, fame, respect, the chance to work on exciting things, loyal and supportive employees, collaborating colleagues, even friendship and love—comes from *other people*. Success, no matter how you define it, is attainable only by persuading another person—a boss, a client, a colleague, a subordinate, a friend or loved one—to give you what you want.

Sustained passion is a scarce, fragile phenomenon.

Understanding people—one-by-one, not in the mass— and how they react to each one of us an individual, is not an optional skill. It is an essential skill.

That doesn't make any of this *easy*. Most of us received training for—and development of—our logical, rational and analytical skills. But few of us have been substantially helped in the development of our interpersonal, psychological, emotional, political, social or sociological skills.

If we are truly to distinguish ourselves as individuals or institutions, we must make the investments in our "diet and exercise" program that will help us achieve excellence in this area of our lives.

However, the conclusion is, I believe, even stronger than that. I believe that it is only when we truly care (for those we serve, for those we work with) that we find the self-discipline to stay with the program. Caring for those we deal with is not only the outcome—the differentiation that gives us our success—but it is also the means.

PRINCIPLES

The third ingredient that helps people and organizations execute their strategies and achieve their goals is a sincere belief in a set of principles.

As I have done in earlier chapters of this book, I have in the past tended to preface my remarks about such things as caring for your people and for your clients by saying: "These are not moral points. They are just good business tactics that will get you more of what you want."

I no longer try to say it that way. It has become increasingly clear

No matter what you want in life, what you want to obtain—riches, fame, respect, the chance to work on exciting things, loyal and supportive employees, collaborating colleagues, even friendship and love— comes from other people.

that, as noted in chapter 1 and have seen repeatedly throughout this book, people who are acting on principle are much more likely to get done what they say they will do than will those who are doing those things solely in pursuit of future rewards.

Perhaps more importantly, men and women who act on principle and, more importantly, are believed to be acting on deeply held principle, attract customers, subordinates, and colleagues. Whether people know your principles and trust you is a major determinant of how they are going to respond to you.

If I understand and trust your ideology, and have confidence that you will live by it, then we can build one type of working relationship. Conversely, if I cannot understand you or do not trust you to live by a clear set of principles, then we may have a transaction, but not a relationship.

The same holds true, as we have seen in this book, at the managerial and organizational level. The most effective organizations are those that are held together by shared and enforced principles, values, and standards. But organizations that have the courage to live by their declared standards are rare—because of the Fat Smoker syndrome.

TWO OUT OF THREE AIN'T BAD? OR IS IT?

Do you really need all three of the elements: passion, people skills, and principles? I'm convinced that in life, careers, and business you do require all three.

If you have both passion and an understanding of how people work, but no fixed principles, then I think you are dangerous. You'll seduce a lot of people to your side, but you'll end up fooling them or betraying them. You'll be an exploiter.

> Men and women who act on principle and, more importantly, are believed to be acting on deeply held principle, attract customers, subordinates, and colleagues.

If you have passion and principles, but no understanding of

how people work, you'll also draw a lot of people to your side, but it will all come to naught. Without an understanding of people, you'll neither build an organization nor earn clients' and customers' trust. You'll be a firebrand.

If you have principles and an understanding of people, but no passion, you'll be righteous but ineffective.

Is any one of these elements more important than another? No. As my wife, Kathy, points out, the most important ingredient in any recipe is the one you forgot to put in!

Bibliography

Blanchard, Kenneth and Spencer Johnson, *The One Minute Manager* (Harper Collins Business, Rev. Ed., 2000).

Carnegie, Dale, *How to Win Friends and Influence People* (Simon & Schuster, 1936).

Cialdini, Robert, *Influence* (Quill, 1984).

Collins, James, *Good to Great* (Harper Business, 2001).

Coens, Tom and Mary Jenkins, *Abolishing Performance Appraisals: Why They Backfire and What to do Instead* (Berrett-Koehler, 2000).

Davenport, Thomas, *Thinking for a Living* (Harvard Business School Press, 2005).

Friedes, Peter, *The 2R Manager* (Jossey-Bass, 2002).

"Goldman's Secret", *The Economist*, April 29, 2006.

Green, Charles, *Trust-Based Selling* (McGraw-Hill, 2005).

Knee, Jonathan, *The Accidental Investment Banker* (Oxford, 2006).

Kohn, Alfie, *Punished by Rewards* (Mariner Books, 1999).

Kouzes, James and Barry Posner, *The Leadership Challenge*, (3rd edition, Jossey-Bass, 2002).

McKenna, Patrick and David Maister, *First Among Equals* (The Free Press, 2002).

Maister, David, *Managing the Professional Service Firm* (The Free Press, 1993).

Maister, David, *True Professionalism* (The Free Press, 1997).

Maister, David, Charles Green and Robert Galford, *The Trusted Advisor* (The Free Press, 2000).

Maister, David, *Practice What You Preach* (The Free Press, 2001).

Maister, David, "Meeting Goals" at *www.davidmaister.com*.

Maister, David and Lois Kelly, "Marketing is a Conversation" at *www.davidmaister.com.*

Mitreanu, Cristian, "Is Strategy a Bad Word?" *MIT Sloan Management Review*, Winter 2006, Vol. 47, No. 2, p. 96.

Mourkogiannis, Nikos, *Purpose: The Starting Point of Great Companies* (Palgrave Macmillan, 2006).

Pfeffer, Jeffrey and Robert Sutton, *The Knowing-Doing Gap* (Harvard Business School Press, 2000).

Skinner, Wickham, "The Focused Factory", *Harvard Business Review.*

Sommer, Brian, "The Lessons of Andersen" at *www.servicessafari.com.*

Welch, Jack and Suzy Welch, *Winning* (Collins, 2005).

Yutan, Lin, trans., *The Wisdom of Confucius* (London, 1958).

Acknowledgements

My gratitude goes to the three people who coauthored chapters in this book: Jack Walker ("The One-Firm Firm Revisited"), Patrick McKenna ("Managing the Multidimensional Firm") and Lois Kelly who coauthored the article "Marketing is a Conversation", from which the opening section of "The Friendship Strategy" is taken.

Chapter 17 ("The Trouble with Lawyers") was originally published in the April 2006 issue of *The American Lawyer.* Many thanks to them for thinking up a better title!

A number of readers served me by reviewing the original drafts of the articles on which this book is based. My most frequent reviewers were my former co-authors Patrick McKenna and Charles Green and they deserve special thanks. Among the many other people to whom I owe thanks are Ron Baker, Edmund Brady, Jay Bertram, Peter Byers, Rick Carter, Jordan Furlong, Joseph Heyison, Terry Jansen, Ed Kless, Drew Marshall, Morris Panner, Ronald Pol, Dick Tyler, Barry White, Hyokon Zhiang, and too many others I probably have forgotten to mention. The many active and loyal supporters of my blog (*www.davidmaister.com/blog*) also made contributions which significantly influenced my thinking.

I have been exceedingly fortunate in working with the team at stresslimitdesign, led by Justin Evans and Colin Vernon, who not only built and ran a highly interactive web presence for both my wife's business and mine, but have helped to shepherd the contents of this book from initial conception, through regular distribution through my online (opt-in) database, and on to the art direction and production of this book. Without them, I would have become obsolescent long ago.

My wife Kathy has always been my support and inspiration. She still is.

About **David Maister**

David Maister is widely acknowledged as one of the world's leading authorities on the management of professional service firms. For twenty-five years he has acted as a consultant to prominent professional firms, around the world, on a wide variety of strategic and managerial issues.

He is the author of the bestselling books *Managing the Professional Service Firm* (1993), *True Professionalism* (1997), *The Trusted Advisor* (2000–coauthor), *Practice What You Preach* (2001), and *First Among Equals* (2002–coauthor). These books have been translated into Arabic, Chinese, Danish, Dutch, Estonian, French, Indonesian, Japanese, Korean, Polish, Russian, Serbo-Croatian, Spanish, and Turkish.

He is very active on-line, regularly publishing new articles on his website. His blog is among the top blogs in the world (on any subject) and, in 2006, he was nominated for a podcaster of the year award.

He spends about 40 percent of his time consulting and speaking in North America, 35 percent in Europe, and 25 percent in the rest of the world.

A native of Great Britain, David holds a bachelor's degree in mathematics, economics, and statistics from the University of Birmingham (1968), a master's degree in operations research from the London School of Economics (1971), and a doctorate in business from the Harvard Business School (1976).

For seven years, he served as a professor on the faculty of the Harvard Business School (1979–85), prior to launching his consulting practice. He lives in Boston, Massachusetts with his wife Kathy, the founder, host, and editorial director of *www.startcooking.com*.

He may be reached at:
Tel: 617-262-5968
Email: david@davidmaister.com

Additional Material
by David Maister

This book is based on articles written between 2005 and 2007. In that period, I wrote (and published on my website) other articles that did not fit the structure and themes of this book. Among them are:

"Marketing is a Conversation" (with Lois Kelly)—which shows how marketing and selling activities can be turned into conversations with clients, rather than one-way communications.

"Geographic Expansion Strategies"—which argues that the expansion strategies of many firms may be precipitous, since the first priority of any business is to differentiate itself in its home markets before trying to "take the show on the road."

"Integrity Impugned"—which explores the appropriate reactions when clients distrust the motives of their providers—and say so!

"Adventures in Modern Marketing"—a description of the lessons learned from my online activities, including my website, blogging, and podcasting.

"Setting Knowledge Free"—a conversation with Steve Rubel about blogging.

In addition to my books, additional articles, podcasts, videos, and blogposts may be found at *www.davidmaister.com*.

Free subscriptions to future articles and other materials may be obtained by visiting *www.davidmaister.com/subscriptions*.

My previous books include:

MANAGING THE PROFESSIONAL SERVICE FIRM (1993)

This book is a comprehensive overview and introduction to professional firms, and is my all-time bestseller, still used as a basic text inside firms to introduce their people to the core principles of firm management. It is divided into seven sections:

- Basic Matters (Organization, Profitability)

- Client Matters

- People Matters

- Management Matters

- Partnership Matters

- Multisite Matters

- Last Thoughts

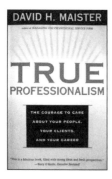

TRUE PROFESSIONALISM (1997)

A collection of 21 articles, this book represents a deeper examination of values and principles in professionalism, client relations, and effective personal leadership. Topics included are "What is Professionalism?", "Why Should I Follow You?", and whether or not firms should guarantee their clients' satisfaction. The book is divided into three sections:

- (Mostly) About You

- (Mostly) About Your Firm

- (Mostly) About Your Clients

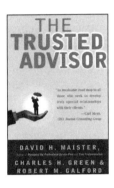

THE TRUSTED ADVISOR (2000)

(with Charles Green and Robert Galford) A worldwide bestseller, this book is written for the individual (novice or senior) who must learn how to build relationships with clients. It has also been extensively used by those who perform an advisory role (HR, legal, marketing, etc.,) inside companies. It is structured into the following sections:

- Perspectives on Trust

- The Structure of Trust Building

- Putting Trust to Work

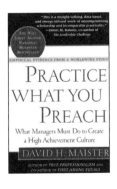

PRACTICE WHAT YOU PREACH (2001)

This is one of those relatively rare studies that provides new evidence on what causes business performance. This data-packed book is divided into two components. Half of the book presents the results of an international study of 139 professional firm offices, formally examining the statistical relationships between employee attitudes and financial outcomes. The other half of the book presents nine case studies of superstar achievement, and what the managers of those operations did to achieve that success.

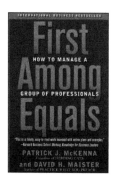

FIRST AMONG EQUALS (2002)

(with Patrick McKenna)

This book was designed to be a practical, hands-on guide for those charged with leading and guiding professional groups from positions of influence rather than traditional command-and-control authority. It is structured into the following components:

- Part One: Getting Ready

- Part Two: Coaching The Individual

- Part Three: Coaching The Team

- Part Four: Building For The Future

All the books described in this section were published by The Free Press, and are available from regular and online bookstores.

INDEX